Paris for Free
(Or Extremely Cheap)

Also by Mark Beffart:

France on the TGV:
How to Use the World's Fastest Train
to Get the Most out of France

Also in this series:

Europe for Free
by Brian Butler

Hawaii for Free
by Frances Carter

London for Free
by Brian Butler

DC for Free
by Brian Butler

The Southwest for Free
by Greg & Mary Jane Edwards

PARIS
FOR FREE
(OR EXTREMELY CHEAP)

REVISED EDITION

**Hundreds of Free &
Inexpensive Things
to Do in Paris**

MARK BEFFART

Mustang Publishing
Memphis, TN

This book is dedicated to all travelers
in search of a bargain—and to my wife Judy,
who has the uncanny ability to find high-quality
merchandise and services at thrift-shop prices,
no matter the location. Her suggestions for bargains
are scattered throughout the book.

Copyright © Mark Beffart.

All rights reserved, including the right of reproduction in whole or in part in any form. Published in the United States of America by Mustang Publishing Company, P.O. Box 3004, Memphis, TN 38173. Manufactured and printed in the U.S.A.

Distributed to the trade by National Book Network, Lanham, MD.

Photographs by Mark Beffart.

Map of Paris © by Let's Go Inc., from the book *Let's Go Europe*, reprinted with permission from St. Martin's Press, Inc.

Library of Congress Cataloging-in-Publication Data
Beffart, Mark, 1953-
    Paris for free (or extremely cheap) : hundreds of free &
inexpensive things to do in Paris / Mark Beffart. -- rev. ed.
        p.   cm.
    ISBN 0-914457-87-X (alk. paper)
    1. Paris (France)--Guidebooks.   2. Suburbs--France--
Paris Region--Guidebooks.   I. Title.
DC708.B43   1997
914.4'36104839--dc21   96-49219
                                                         CIP

Printed on acid-free paper.
10 9 8 7 6 5 4 3 2 1

Acknowledgments

My special thanks to the French Government Tourist Office and *Office du Tourisme de Paris* for the wealth of material they have sent me over the years, to Blaise Bouchand for his translation services and superb tips/quips about Paris (e.g., Parisians call the Eiffel Tower the "Big Woman"), and to the many Parisians I've met who happily supplied information about their city and extended their hospitality and friendliness.

Mark Beffart

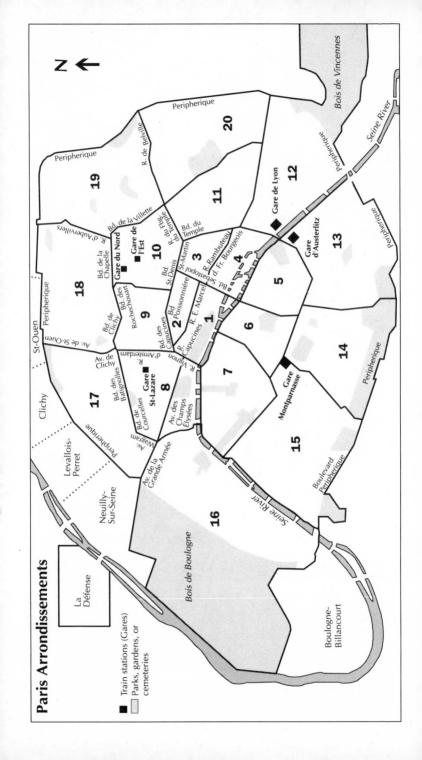

Paris Arrondissements

■ Train stations (Gares)
▨ Parks, gardens, or cemeteries

La Défense

N ←

Peripherique

Bois de Vincennes

Seine River

20

19

11

12

Gare de Lyon

R. de Belville

Bd. de la Villette

R. du Fbg. du temple

Bd. du Temple

Gare du Nord

Gare de l'Est

10

3

R. Rambuteau

R. d. Fr. Bourgeois

4

13

Gare d'Austerlitz

Bd. d'Aubervilliers

St-Martin

Bd. St-Denis

Bd. Poissonnière

Bd. Montmartre

5

18

Bd. de la Chapelle

Bd. de Clichy

Bd. des Rochechouart

9

Bd. des Capucines

2

R. E. Marcel

1

6

Peripherique

St-Ouen

Av. de St-Ouen

R. des Capucines

R. Vignon

R. d'Amsterdam

7

14

Av. de Clichy

Gare St-Lazare

8

Gare Montparnasse

Bd. des Batignolles

Bd. de Courcelles

Av. des Champs Élysées

15

17

Av. Wagram

Boulevard Peripherique

Clichy

Av. de la Grande Armée

Levallois-Perret

Peripherique

Neuilly-Sur-Seine

16

Seine River

Bois de Boulogne

Boulogne-Billancourt

Contents

Introduction

*P*aris is one of the most beautiful and interesting cities in the world, a vibrant metropolis full of adventure, history, and constant activity. As you walk by students in the narrow medieval streets of the Latin Quarter, relax in a Montmartre bistro over *pot-au-feu* and a bottle of vintage wine, or view fascinating art in a Left Bank gallery, the city will capture your emotions like no other. Whether you're a novice or frequent visitor, you'll take home new discoveries and memories that will last a lifetime.

Whatever you hope to find—romance, the avant-garde, historic monuments, gastronomic delights, Gothic cathedrals, grand boulevards, café society, *haute couture*, unparalleled shopping—you can find it in Paris. After all, the City of Light is a city of great reputations. It remains a world leader in art, style, fashion, and cuisine. When a new style or taste gains a following in Paris, it usually sweeps the civilized world.

Paris also defines everything that is France. As the capital and melting pot of the nation, its nearly three million residents (within the city limits; there are another nine million in the suburbs) hail from every region in France, from northernmost Calais to Corsica in the Mediterranean Sea, from the Alps to the Atlantic. It's a city of great ethnic diversity; scattered throughout the city in distinct neighborhoods are North Africans, Asians, and other immigrants from former French colonies, plus contingents of foreign refugees, political dissidents, expatriates, temporary workers, and students. To be in Paris is to know France *and* experience a slice of many other lands.

To the chagrin of its residents and visitors, Paris also bears the reputation of being one of the most expensive cities in the world. *Per diem* costs are often listed at $200 or more, and $125 per night hotels are considered bargains. But *francly* speaking, it doesn't have to be that way. In the following pages, you'll discover a Paris that is inexpensive—even downright cheap.

Using This Book

To navigate Paris for free (or extremely cheap), you need this book.

You don't have to pay admission for everything you "must see." Many of Paris's primary attractions—including the avenue de Champs-Élysées, place des Vosges, Latin Quarter, and Cathédrale de Notre-Dame, plus parts of the Tour Eiffel, Arc de Triomphe, and Centre Georges Pompidou—are free. You can visit churches with some of the best art and architecture in France, relax in parks filled with attractions, explore fascinating graveyards, wander through unique neighborhoods (where you'll encounter monuments at most major crossroads), attend a variety of street markets, walk along the lovely Seine River, and browse the high-fashion stores without ever making a purchase (if you have enough willpower). Further, those museums and attractions that charge an admission fee usually offer one free day per week or half-price admission on specific days.

Arrondissements

Although Paris has the largest city population in France, it is geographically small (no more than six miles between any two points)—a perfect size for reaching your chosen sights on foot or via public transportation. To take advantage of this, this book lists the sights under their *arrondissement* (a city government administrative district, each with its own mayor, city hall, central post office, and police station).

Paris consists of 20 arrondissements. The 1st arrondissement begins on the west half of the Ile de la Cité at the center of Paris. From there, the other arrondissements spiral outward in every direction, ending at the boulevard Périphérique, an express, multi-lane highway that circles the city and separates it from the suburbs. Arrondissements 1-4, 8-12, and 16-20 are located north of the Seine River (Right Bank Paris), with arrondissements 5-7 and 13-15 south of the river (Left Bank Paris). By walking to the sights listed for each arrondissement (instead of jumping all over the city from sight to sight), you'll get a better look at the Paris that residents know. If you take a wrong turn while seeking your next sight, note that arrondissement numbers are posted on street signs.

Each chapter begins by briefly introducing the arrondisse-ment, its major sights, and its boundaries, followed by the most popular free/extremely cheap sights in the area. Since Paris is best seen on foot, notable streets to investigate are included. Each entry, spelled as you will find it in Paris, includes basic information about the sight, plus its street address, nearest Métro/RER station(s) (Paris subway) with its line(s), nearest bus lines, and when applicable, telephone number, hours, and ad-mission fee. Under hours, a notation is made for sights closed on specific days, months, and/or holidays. Sights with no spe-cific notations are closed for all holidays.

Admission and hours are omitted for parks and churches, since most are open similar hours and are free (though some churches charge a fee to visit the crypt, treasury, or belfry). For museums and historic monuments, a notation under the admis-sion section is made for those accepting the **Carte Musées et Monuments** pass. When this is the only listing for admission, it indicates that the museum is expensive, making the pass your cheapest method of entry. (For complete information about this pass, see the chapter *Miscellaneous Paris Bargains*.) Most sights charging an entry fee offer free, half-price, or reduced tickets to people age 18-24 and 60+. Fees for children under 18 are gen-erally cheaper than regular admission.

To plan a tour around specific sights, refer to the Index. For more free/extremely cheap sights in Paris, examine the chapters *Miscellaneous Paris Bargains* and *Annual Free (or Extremely Cheap) Events in Paris and Its Suburbs*. All RER lines—and some Métro and bus lines—extend into the suburbs, so *Paris Suburbs for Free (or Extremely Cheap)* lists easily accessible sights on the outskirts of the city.

Defining "Extremely Cheap"

Of course, "extremely cheap" is a relative term. For some, a night at the Hôtel Ritz for less than $500 is a bargain. For oth-ers, any meal over $10 is a luxury. After polling several inde-pendent travelers with moderate incomes, we based "extreme-ly cheap" on the guidelines shown below, using a conversion rate of six francs per dollar as a standard. (Conversion rates have fluctuated between 4.85F-7F per dollar during the last five years.) If the rate jumps to 10 francs per dollar as in 1985, you'll be in bargain heaven.

Museums/Historic Sights: 22F or less. A few exceptions are made for museums like the Louvre that require several hours to view properly, for multi-purpose sights, and for those sights offering extra-day ticket validity and multiple museums for one price.

Private Gardens/Parks: 11F or less.

Sporting Events/Concerts/Theater: 36F or less.

Movies: 24F or less per movie.

Recreation (bowling, dancing, swimming, tennis, etc.): 28F or less per game, 19F or less by the hour.

Disclaimer

Although the information in this book was accurate at press time, some details might change. For example, more and more, Paris museums are changing their free admission days to half-price days. And with inflation, you can almost bet prices will rise. But compared to everything else, the sights listed herein will still be bargains. Public transportation routes and prices are always subject to change. Neither the author nor the publisher assume any liability for any problem you may encounter due to an inaccuracy in this book.

If you find a free or extremely cheap sight in Paris that is not mentioned in this book, or if you think one of the listed sights no longer qualifies for inclusion, let us know so we can change the next edition. Please write to *Paris for Free*, c/o Mustang Publishing, P.O. Box 3004, Memphis, TN 38173 USA.

Paris Essentials

When you arrive in Paris, you will enter a culture with a set of rules and customs that may be quite different from those in your country. Unless you are a frequent visitor, you'll probably experience some form of cultural inadequacy—beginning with the French language, the 24-hour clock system, and other cultural nuances. The following tips and suggestions will help make your Paris vacation more comfortable.

When to Go
In general, the best seasons to visit Paris are the spring and fall, when the temperature is usually mild and the tourist population is manageable. May, when the flowers are in full bloom, is an especially pretty month, but it also has the most holidays to plan around. Though much colder and with constant chance for rain or snow, the winter has more cultural events, fewer tourists, and discounted hotel rooms. In the peak season of June to September, expect large crowds at the major sights and higher prices. If possible, avoid Paris in August, when many Parisians take their vacations and close their businesses for the month.

Average Paris Monthly Temperatures (in Fahrenheit)

Jan	Feb	Mar	Apr	May	June	July	Aug	Sept	Oct	Nov	Dec
43°	45°	51°	60°	62°	74°	76°	78°	70°	62°	53°	46°

National Holidays
An important consideration when planning your trip to Paris are French national holidays (*jours fériés*), when most businesses close for the day, including many restaurants. Train stations, airports, hotels, and public transportation operate with a minimum staff. Banks often close the afternoon *before* the holiday. When the holiday occurs on a Thursday, Friday, Monday, or Tuesday, expect longer closures, as people combine the holiday

and weekend with their vacation schedule. The 13 national holidays are January 1, Easter Sunday (in late March or early April), Easter Monday, May 1 (*La Fête du Travail*—French Labor Day), May 8 (Victory in Europe Day), Ascension Day (40 days after Easter), Pentecost Sunday (seventh Sunday after Easter), Pentecost Monday, July 14 (Bastille Day), August 15 (Assumption of the Virgin Mary), November 1 (All Saints' Day), November 11 (Armistice Day), and December 25 (Christmas).

Free Information

In the United States, the best source for free information on Paris is the **French Government Tourist Office**. You can call their "France on Call" hot line at 900-990-0040 (50 cents per minute) or contact them at the following locations:

- 444 Madison Ave., 16th Floor, New York, NY 10022; phone 212-838-7800.

- 676 North Michigan Ave., Suite 3360, Chicago, IL 60611; phone 312-337-6301

- 2305 Cedar Springs Blvd., Dallas, TX 75201; phone 214-720-4010

- 9454 Wilshire Blvd., Beverly Hills, CA 90212; phone 213-271-6665.

In Canada, their addresses are 1981 Ave. McGill College, Tour Esso #490, Montreal, PQ H3A 2W9 (phone 514-288-4723) and 30 St-Patrick St. #700, Toronto, ON M5T 3A3 (phone 416-593-6427). In England, the address is 178 Piccadilly, London W1V 0AL (phone 01-629-9376). In Australia, the address is B&P Building 12th Floor, 12 Castlereagh St., Sydney, NSW 2000 (phone 02-231-52-44).

For *Office du Tourisme* addresses in Paris, see chapters 7, 8, 10, 12, 13, and 15.

Paris Airports

International flights arrive at the **Aéroport Charles-de-Gaulle**, 15.5 miles northeast of Paris, and the **Aéroport d'Orly**, eight miles south of the city. Both airports are well served by a variety of public transportation to Paris, as noted below.

To Paris from Aéroport Charles-de-Gaulle (CDG)

Roissyrail—Combining speed and economy, the best way to travel into Paris from CDG is by Roissyrail, an RER train (line B) with stops at the Gare du Nord, Châtelet/Les Halles, St-Michel/Notre-Dame, Luxembourg, Port Royal, Denfert/Rochereau, and Cité Universitaire stations. To reach the Roissy RER station, board the free *navette* (shuttle bus) in front of Gate 28 at Aérogare 1 (the terminal for trans-Atlantic flights) or Gate 5 at Aérogare 2 (the terminal for Air France and all other flights). Roissyrail costs 46F for a second-class ticket and 68F for first class. Trains run every 15 minutes from 5am-11:59pm and take 25 minutes to reach the Gare du Nord.

Public Buses—Three other inexpensive—but less direct than Roissyrail—methods of transportation into Paris from CDG are public buses #350 and #351. Operating from 6am-11:51pm, both buses leave every 20-30 minutes from Aérogare 1 at the RATP (R*égie Autonome des Transports Parisiens,* operator of the Paris RER, Métro, and bus systems) sign on the *Boutiquaire* level and from Gates A5 and B6 at Aérogare 2. The trip takes 50 minutes during normal traffic and costs six second-class Métro tickets or 45F. (Ticket machines are near the exit gate.) Before you board, keep in mind that public buses lack luggage space, make many stops, and are usually crowded. Bus #350's final stops are at the Gare du Nord and Gare de l'Est, while #351 terminates at place de la Nation, where you'll find a large Métro station (lines 1, 2, 6, 9, and A). The Roissybus departs every 15 minutes from Aérogare 2 to the Paris Opéra-Garnier in central Paris (9th arrondissement). It runs from 5:45am-11pm and costs 40F. Average travel time is 45 minutes.

Air France Bus—Excluding taxis, the most convenient and comfortable way to travel into Paris from CDG is on the Air France bus. Anyone can ride it, not just Air France passengers. It leaves every 15 minutes from Gate 36 at Aérogare 1 and every 20 minutes from Gates A5-6, B6-7 at Aérogare 2, with stops near the Arc de Triomphe and Palais des Congrés (Porte Maillot). The modern, air-conditioned buses have lots of luggage space, cost 55F, and run from 6:15am-9pm. (Discounts are available for small groups; four people can travel on one ticket for 187F.) Another bus, taking one hour and costing 65F, travels to the Gare Montparnasse. You can buy tickets from the driver or the ticket booth at Palais des Congrès.

Taxi—A taxi ride from CDG to the center of Paris costs 250F-300F and takes 35 minutes or longer, depending on the traffic and your driver. After 8pm, the fare will be up to 30% higher. When you enter the taxi, be sure the last passenger's fare has been removed from the meter, lest it be added to your fare. Also, note that some cabs have a three-passenger limit and charge for extra suitcases.

To Paris from Aéroport d'Orly

Orlyrail—The Aéroport d'Orly is linked with Paris through the RER system, with stops at the Gare d'Austerlitz, St-Michel/Notre Dame, Musée d'Orsay, Invalides, and Champ de Mars/Tour Eiffel. Free *navettes* (shuttle buses) depart from *Orly-Sud* (international flights) Gate H and *Orly-Ouest* (domestic flights) Gate F to the Pont de Rungis RER station (line C).

Orlyrail trains run every 15 minutes from 5:35am-11:17pm, take 35 minutes to reach the Gare d'Austerlitz, and cost 28F for a second-class ticket, 42.5F for first class.

OrlyVal—The OrlyVal train, from its own station (elevated track above the taxi lanes) at both *Orly-Sud* and *Orly-Ouest*, travels a short distance northwest of Orly to the Antony RER station, where you transfer to the RER line B train for travel into Paris. It has the same stops as Roissyrail (in reverse order), plus direct service to CDG. OrlyVal trains operate from 6:30am-9:15pm Mon-Sat and 7am-10:55pm on Sunday, run every seven minutes, and cost 54F (includes transfer to Métro line), no matter where you get off inside Paris. It takes 19 minutes to reach the Cité Universitaire station, 30 minutes to Châtelet/Les Halles.

Orlybus—The express Orlybus, which has only four stops, travels to place Denfert-Rochereau every 15 minutes from 6am-11pm, takes 30 minutes during normal traffic, and costs 30F. It departs from *Orly-Sud*, gate H, platform 4.

JetBus—Slightly quicker and cheaper than the Orlybus, the privately-owned JetBus travels from Orly in 12 minutes to the Ville-juif/Louis Aragon station, the southern terminus of Métro line 7. Since JetBus has longer operating hours and better frequency, take it if your hotel is near this Métro line. Line 7 stops include Jussieu (5th arrondissement), Pont Neuf, Châtelet, Palais Royal/Musée du Louvre, Pyramides, Opéra, Chausée d'Antin/La

Fayette, and Gare de l'Est. The JetBus runs every 12 minutes from 5:48am-11:36pm and costs 21F.

Air France Bus—Air France also provides bus transportation into Paris from Orly, with stops at the Porte d'Orleans, Gare Montparnasse, Duroc, and Invalides Métro stations. Buses leave every 12 minutes from *Orly-Sud* Gate J and *Orly-Ouest* Gate E, take 30 minutes in normal traffic to reach the Invalides station, run from 5:50am-11:10pm, and cost 40F per ticket. As with the Air France buses from CDG, reduced rates are available for small groups traveling together, and you can buy tickets from the driver.

Other Public Bus Options—If your hotel is in the 13th arrondissement, consider traveling from Orly into Paris on bus #183A to Porte de Choisy. Buses #131, #183, and #285 travel from the Pont de Rungis RER station to Porte d'Italie. Both stops have stations for Métro line 7. These buses cost four Métro tickets.

Taxi—A taxi from Orly to the center of Paris costs 150F-200F and takes 25 minutes or longer, depending on the traffic and your driver.

Paris Public Transportation

Métro—The best way to travel quickly throughout Paris is to use the Métro, an elaborate subway system with 15 lines, 124 miles of tunnels, and 368 stations. No destination in Paris is very far from a Métro stop. If you combine the Métro with RER lines A-D (suburban express trains that make limited stops within the city), you can go from one end of the city to the other (and some suburbs) in a few minutes. Compared to other subways in the world, the Paris Métro is fast, efficient, inexpensive, reasonably safe (beware of pickpockets), and easy to negotiate. All sights in this book are keyed to a Métro station and line (though you'll have to determine any transfers you might need).

Métro trains run from 5:30am-1am and cost 8F per ride. (First-class cars were discontinued in 1991 but may be reinstated.) A ticket entitles you to ride for as long as you please (until you exit a station), with multiple transfers to other lines (but not to buses) included. RER trains accept Métro tickets for travel within the Paris city limits (zones 1 and 2). For suburban destinations, you must purchase an individual ticket.

For a short stay in Paris, buy a *carnet* (10 loose tickets) for 46F or a *Formule 1* pass, which is valid for one day of unlimited travel on the Métro, RER, buses, and selected SNCF trains (30F for zones 1 and 2—equal to nearly seven Métro tickets when you buy a *carnet*). If you're staying longer than four days, buy a weekly *Coupon Hebdomadaire* (a.k.a. *Coupon Semaine* or *Coupon Jaune* for 72F (zones 1 and 2) or the monthly *Coupon Mensuel* (243F for zones 1 and 2), all valid for unlimited travel. Some of the passes, which resemble and are used the same way as a regular ticket, require a *Carte Orange* (an ID card for which you supply a passport-size photograph), obtained the first time you purchase a pass. If you have regular business in the suburbs, there are weekly and monthly passes for all eight transportation zones.

The *Paris-Visite* pass pushed upon tourists is a bad deal unless you plan to spend a lot of time on public transportation, go to the suburbs a lot, and take advantage of all their discounts (20% admission price reductions to a few museums and tours). The passes offer unlimited travel in zones 1-3 and cost 70F for two days, 105F for three days consecutive use, and 165F for five days. There are also two-, three-, and five-day passes for travel within zones 1-5, costing 170F, 230F, and 315F respectively.

Métro stations are identified by signs with a large letter "M" inside a circle, the word *Métro*, or the word *Métropolitain* written in scroll letters over the entrance. For the RER, look for its letters inside a blue circle. Inside each Métro entrance, there are ticket booths, mini-shopping malls in the larger stations, a *plan du quartier* map detailing streets and buildings surrounding the station, and large Métro system maps.

Free pocket-size maps (*Petit Plan de Paris*) showing the Paris Métro, RER, and bus networks are available at the ticket counter. Some stations have electronic boards to show the route you need to take. Punch the button for your destination and the board lights up, showing any transfers needed. Transfer stations where lines intersect are indicated on the maps by a circle.

To ride the Métro, insert the narrow ticket into the turnstile slot to open the gate. Be sure to retrieve your ticket when it shoots out the top of the turnstile. Sometimes Métro officials will ask for it to verify that you are not riding for free, and you'll need it to exit through the gates at RER stations. There's a 150F fine if you are caught without a ticket.

From the turnstile area, or when exiting any Métro car for a transfer, look for the orange signs saying *Correspondence*, the interconnecting passages that lead you to the correct line. After following the sign to the line you want, look for a *Direction* sign to guide you to the correct platform. The names on the *Direction* signs are the last stops for the line. For example, if you are at place de la Concorde, served by line 1, and want to get to place de la Bastille in east Paris, you would travel in the direction of Château-de-Vincennes (east terminus of the line), departing at the Bastille station. When you reach your destination, follow the *Sortie* signs to the exits.

Buses—Paris also has an elaborate bus system, which accepts the same tickets used on the Métro. The shelters with red and yellow circular signs on the street are bus stops. Each stop posts a route map showing the number of tickets you'll need for your journey, bus transfers, timetables, and other bus information. Most buses operate from 6am-8:30pm. (A few run later into the evening.) There's limited service on Sundays and holidays (when some buses don't run at all). All buses with three-digit numbers go into the suburbs, and there are ten early morning *Noctambus* routes (A-H, J, & R) operating from 1am-5am, with their first stop at place du Châtelet. For late-night workers (and revelers), these buses are a blessing.

After entering the bus, stick your Métro ticket in the validating machine by the entrance door. Some trips will require additional tickets, since buses are accessed by sections as listed on the bus route sign. If you have a pass, show it to the driver. Do **not** stick the pass into the machine, which will punch a hole through its metal strip and invalidate it!

Especially with a weekly or monthly pass, the public bus is a cheap way to tour many parts of Paris that would otherwise take too long by foot. Interesting bus routes are listed under the *Miscellaneous Paris Bargains* chapter.

Business Hours

Paris uses the 24-hour clock, starting with 1am or 0100 hours (also listed as 100 or 1.00 hours). Midnight is 2400 hours. So, to figure the pm time, subtract 12 from the listed hour. (Example: If a store's closing time is 1830 hours, it closes at 6:30pm.) Paris businesses usually keep the following hours:

Banks are open Mon-Fri 9am-4:30pm and may be closed

during the lunch hour. Currency exchange offices in airports and train stations are open every day for long hours, some even on national holidays.

Cafés open daily between 6am and noon and close anytime from the mid-evening hours to 2am. Some are closed on Sundays.

Bistros, **brasseries**, and some **restaurants** serve lunch daily noon-2:30pm. Some offer supper 7:30pm-10:30pm, though it's more fashionable to eat after 8:30pm. Some are closed on Sundays.

Churches/cathedrals are open daily 7am-7pm. Do not explore a church when a service is in progress.

National **museums** are open Wed-Mon 9:30-noon and 2pm-5:30pm. City museums are open the same hours Tue-Sun. Private museums have their own hours. Very popular museums like the Louvre do not close for lunch, and some museums are open one or more nights per week. Historic sights and monuments have similar hours.

Public **parks/gardens** with locked gates are open 8am-sunset. Unlocked parks/gardens are open 24 hours, but be cautious at night.

Post Offices (P.T.T.) are open Mon-Fri 8am-7pm and Sat 8am-noon. The main Paris post office at 52 rue du Louvre is open 24 hours.

Retail shops and **service businesses** are open Mon-Sat 9am-noon and 2pm-6pm. Stores selling food have longer hours, often 7am-8pm and sometimes Sunday 8am-noon. Department stores and essential service businesses will remain open during lunch hours. Street markets are open Tues-Sat 7:30am-1pm. Some markets open again from 4pm-7:30pm, and some operate on Sunday mornings.

Hours for **tourist information offices** are listed under the Arrondissements.

Train station **ticket booths** are open Mon-Sat 6am-10pm, with slightly shorter hours and limited service on Sundays.

Dining Establishments

Bar: Emphasizes alcoholic drinks, snack foods, and sometimes musical entertainment. They rarely serve coffee and full course meals.

Bistro: A bistro serves basic, home-style food like *pot-au-feu* (roast beef simmered with vegetables), *poulet rôti* (roasted chicken), and *tarte tatin* (caramelized upside-down apple pie) in hearty portions in a traditional setting. The decor and cuisine will not be fancy, but you will leave full.

Brasserie: A *brasserie* (brewery) specializes in German-style dishes like *choucroute et saucisse* (sauerkraut and sausage), with a good selection of beer and white wines. Many locations are a combination café, beer hall, and stylish restaurant.

Buffet: Usually found in railroad stations and airports, the selection ranges from basic fare to exceptional cuisine, from cheap to expensive.

Café: Paris is famous for its cafés, especially on the Left Bank. They have long hours, so you can get breakfast, light meals throughout the day and evening, and all forms of beverages.

Cafeteria: Quick and basic ready-to-eat meals with several choices of food—the same as in North America.

Crêperie: A café or small restaurant serving primarily meat-filled, vegetable, and dessert crêpes.

Fast Food: Paris has been overrun with American franchises (McDonald's, Burger King, Pizza Hut, etc.), and French-owned establishments operating under the same principles (inexpensive fast food and drink in self-serve, sterile settings).

Restaurants: A restaurant only serves meals at set times, usually requires reservations, offers a more varied menu with better cuisine, and is more formal and stylish in decor, food preparation, and service. There are restaurants in Paris in all price ranges and types of cuisine, from regional French fare to sushi bars. The chain restaurant concept, where you get the same kind of food for the same price from several different locations, has gotten more popular in Paris in recent years. *Batifol*, with bistro-style food, is one of the better establishments.

Salons de Thé: More sedate and stylish than a café or wine bar, tea salons are primarily places to have dessert over a cup of coffee or tea. Many are extensions of pastry shops.

Wine Bar: Resembling a café, it emphasizes wine by the glass or bottle, with light meals and platters of cheese.

French Floor Numbering System

The floors in Paris buildings are numbered differently from those in other countries. The street level or ground floor is essentially floor zero or the *rez-de-chaussée*, marked on elevators as "RC". The first floor or *premier étage* is the second floor up from the street. The basement is called the *sous-sol* ("SS" on elevators).

Hotels

Inexpensive hotels are available throughout Paris at less than 180F for a double room (slightly less for singles)—if you are willing to take a mediocre room and reduced amenities (thin towels, no elevator, no telephone, no television, old and dusty furniture, sagging mattresses, peeling wallpaper, and back alley views). Rooms without a toilet, tub, and/or shower are always cheaper. Also, avoid the breakfast, which will add 20F-30F to the daily price. If you travel light, a few better hotels have tiny rooms with complete amenities in the above price range. Hotels catering to students and those in non-tourist neighborhoods offer the cheapest lodging. All 0-3 star hotels are required to post their prices.

If you're on a strict budget and don't mind noisy, dormitory-style living, stay at a hostel, which charges less than 100F per night. Before leaving the U.S., consider joining Hostelling International (P.O. Box 37613, Washington, D.C. 20013-7613), which has two locations in Paris.

Check-out time for Paris hotels is noon. Since rooms go fast at popular establishments, the earlier you arrive, the better chance you'll have for a good room. If you expect to arrive after 6pm and do not have a pre-paid reservation, the hotel will hold a room reserved with a major credit card. As a last resort, if you can't find a hotel, the Office de Tourisme will find you a room for a slight surcharge.

Maps

Although Paris is geographically small, its maze of narrow streets makes it easy to get turned around. If you plan to do heavy touring and random street exploration, buy a detailed map, since the maps given away by the Office du Tourisme list only the primary streets.

Three excellent maps in book form (with an alphabetized

index for every street in Paris) are Michelin's *Paris Index Plan,*
Paris by Arrondissement, and *Plan de Paris.* Although you can
order them from any bookstore, they are considerably cheaper
in Paris. *Paris by Arrondissement* sells for $19.95 in the U.S., 32-
38F in a Paris bookstore.

Money

The basic unit of French currency is the *franc,* which breaks
down into 100 *centimes.* Coins come in 5, 10, 20, and 50 cen-
time denominations, plus ½, 1, 2, 5, 10, and 20 franc units.
Paper money comes in 10, 20, 50, 100, 200, and 500 franc bills.

Traveler's checks by American Express, Citicorp, MasterCard,
Thomas Cook, Visa, and others are available in francs in the
paper money denominations. All the vendors have locations in
Paris to replace your checks in case of theft or loss.

Credit cards by American Express, Diner's Card, MasterCard
(known as *EuroCard* in France), and Visa (*Carte Bleue*) are
accepted at many hotels, restaurants, shops, and Métro stations.
For instant currency, credit and bank access cards are accepted
in most Paris banks' ATMs (especially BNP, Crédit Lyonnais,
and Crédit Mutuél).

Parisians

The experienced traveler to Paris gets one frequent question:
"Are Parisians really rude and arrogant?" The answer is no—
most of the time.

First, one must view Paris as a Parisian. It's a fast-paced city
like New York and Los Angeles, with similar problems of pollu-
tion, crime, and high living expenses. Parisians, who boast of
their ability to thrive in this atmosphere, see themselves as
being the best at everything in France, sometimes snubbing fel-
low French from the provinces as much as any foreigner.

On the flip side, I've met Parisians who have invited me into
their homes to meet their family and share a meal, given me
gifts, and paid for my meal at restaurants. Shopkeepers have
gone overboard to help me make the right selection; waiters
have patiently explained the menu and freely offered advice;
students have eagerly attempted their English in return for my
answering their questions about America; and even civil serv-
ants at ticket booths have saved me money by offering a better
route and little-known discounts.

The key to a positive Paris experience is **your** attitude. Go with an open mind and a healthy dose of patience. And above all, don't let the tiny percentage of rude people, whom you will find anywhere in the world, ruin your vacation.

Parlez-vous Français?
If possible, learn to speak some French before you leave. Just trying to communicate·in French, even if you lack the proper accent and verb conjugations, will make Parisians more receptive to you. Just make sure you don't order baked dog (*chien rôti*) in a restaurant or say something derogatory or vulgar.

Public Rest Rooms
Public rest rooms, identified by the letters "W.C." (water closet) or the word *Toilettes,* are available in large Métro stations, train stations, parks, department stores, and museums (often just inside the entrance). Don't expect modern fixtures or free use at every location; they vary from the primitive hole-in-the-floor to ultra-modern plumbing, and some charge 1-4F. Privacy also varies widely. Unisex facilities are common; men and women enter through the same entrance, with the facilities separated by a divider. In older buildings, both sexes share the same room, sinks, and toilets. The space capsule-like *Toilettes,* on some street corners, cost 2F to enter. A café will also let you use its W.C., though it's proper to buy some food or drink before using the facilities.

Telephones & Minitel
Most public telephones in Paris operate with a *télécarte,* France Telecom's telephone debit card. Resembling a credit card, it is inserted in a slot on the telephone, which deducts the cost of the call from your card. Cards are available in 25-, 50- and 120-franc units from post offices, cafés, magazine kiosks, train stations, and Métro station ticket booths.

To make a call in Paris, dial the eight-digit number. To reach the U.S., dial 19, listen for the dial tone, then dial 1 (the country code), the area code, and the number. To get an English-speaking operator in France, dial 19-3311 or 19-0011 for an American AT&T operator. A one-minute call to the U.S. costs about 8F.

Minitel, a small computer connected through the telephone,

offers access to many services in France for information and for ordering products. If you're a current events junkie, it has on-screen newspapers and stories from English-language magazines. Minitel is available to the public in large post offices and libraries. If you can't read French, access an English directory by punching 3614 on the keyboard, wait for the beep, then press the Connection button and type ED. Minitel costs 37 centimes-4F per minute (depending on the service) and accepts *télécartes* for payment.

Value-Added Tax (VAT)
Prices in Paris appear higher than in the U.S. because France adds a value-added tax into the price of all products and services. Gasoline has a whopping 78% tax, but most goods and services fall in the 5.5%-22% range. Luxury items like perfume are assessed at the 33% rate. You can get a VAT refund only when 1) you spend 2,000 or more francs at a single store, 2) your purchases are taken out of France, and 3) your stay in France does not exceed six months. Stores have VAT refund forms and instructions.

Miscellaneous Paris Bargains

This chapter lists free and extremely cheap sights, entertainment, and other bargains that don't fit under a specific arrondissement—plus general suggestions on how to navigate Paris on the cheap.

Architecture, Art, Culture, & Entertainment

AlloConcerts
For 24-hour information (in French) about free concerts in Paris, phone 42-76-50-00.

Architecture & Art
No matter what Paris street you follow, you'll see interesting architecture and art—all free for viewing from the street. Wall paintings adorn some of the modern buildings; statues, modern sculpture, and fountains grace parks and traffic intersections; interesting architectural accents highlight most buildings in town. The point is, you can see a ton of free culture just by being observant as you walk.

Art Galleries
You can view art for free at the hundreds of art galleries scattered throughout the city. The largest concentration is found in the Left Bank arrondissements 5-7 (especially the St-Germain-des-Prés district), the area surrounding the Centre Georges Pompidou, throughout the ritzy 8th arrondissement, and in the 11th and 12th arrondissements near place de la Bastille, where many artists have moved for cheap rents.

Carte Musées et Monuments

This pass gives you immediate admission to the permanent collections of 65 museums and monuments in Paris and the Ile de France region. It costs 70F for one day, 140F for three consecutive days, and 200F for five consecutive days. When you go to popular museums like the Louvre and Orsay, it will save you time because it lets you skip the long ticket line. It's also a good bargain if you visit several museums per day.

However, the three- and five-day passes are good only for consecutive days, and the clock starts ticking the first time you use the pass. So, if you plan to see only a few museums and spend a long time in each, you might do better just to buy a ticket at the museum.

Since most museums are open from 9am-5pm, plan well so you get your money's worth. If a museum you want to see is open at night, pick that day for your pass, since you'll get an additional three to five hours for museum-hopping.

Museums and monuments accepting the pass are indicated in the arrondissements sections under *Admission*. When the "Carte" is the only listing under *Admission*, it means the museum is expensive (by this book's standards), making the pass your cheapest method of entry.

The pass is available from the Office du Tourisme headquarters at 127 avenue des Champs-Élysées, all participating museums, Métro ticket booths, and Musée & Compagnie (49 rue Étienne-Marcel). ***Note:*** The pass is not valid for temporary exhibitions offered by the museums.

Cemeteries

Some of the best sculpture and art lies in Paris's cemeteries as tomb decor. Some you might want to explore are listed in the arrondissement chapters.

Classical/Traditional Music

Several museums, parks, squares, and churches offer free organ recitals, choirs, and concerts. Outdoor concerts are usually held only during the summer months.

Church Art

Some of the best examples of art, architecture, stained glass, and Old World craftsmanship are available for free viewing in

the hundreds of Paris churches. The ones with the most interesting architecture and interiors are noted in the chapters.

Church Concerts

For information about concerts in churches, call 40-30-10-13.

Cultural Centers

Nearly every developed country has a cultural center in Paris
devoted to helping and promoting its citizens, especially those
working in the fine arts in France. Most centers offer free or
extremely cheap events including concerts, lectures, and art
exhibits. Many also have libraries, where you can catch up on
current events and read other literature. The most prominent
cultural centers are discussed in the arrondissement chapters,
but don't be afraid to visit others not listed.

Graffiti

With graffiti-makers like Keith Haring, Futura 2000, and others
in New York City gaining artistic fame (some deserving, some
not), graffiti has taken Paris by storm—much to the dismay of
shop owners and government officials, who find many walls
and Métro cars covered with it. Although most graffiti is puerile
vandalism, occasionally some is truly refined art. And in case
you're tempted to partake, Paris does have an anti-graffiti ordi-
nance with stiff jail terms and fines.

Métro Art & Entertainment

A number of Métro stations have exhibits of art (copies) or inter-
estingly painted walls, ceilings, and stairwells. Some of the best
are Abbesses (Métro line 12; painted stairwell), Assemblée-
Nationale (12; painted walls and ceilings), Bastille (1; tiled walls
with historic scenes), Chausée d'Antin-La Fayette (7, 9; frescoed
ceiling), Louvre-Rivoli (1; art reproductions), and Varenne (13;
copies of Rodin sculpture).

There's always a variety of interesting, impromptu entertainment in the Métro stations, including classical and rock music,
poetry readings, and my favorite, a puppet show set up at the
end of a car on a late-night ride. Often when someone breaks
into song, others (especially the inebriated) join in as the cho-
rus. Pause to listen for a few minutes and give them a few coins
if you enjoyed the show.

Movies

Although there are nearly 350 commercial movie screens within the Paris city limits, the average cost of a first run movie is 50F. If you love film, you can save money by going to the **Vidéothèque de Paris** (1st arrondissement), **Salle Garance** (4th), **Action Rive Gauche** (5th), and **Cinémathèque Française** (16th). A few theaters run specials and have festivals that let you view several films for one price. If you're staying in Paris for several weeks, join one of the movie clubs offering one free ticket for a specific number of paid admissions. *Cinescope*, bundled into the weekly *Pariscope* (see "Publications" below), gives a complete update on movies in Paris, including over 300 capsule movie reviews.

Music & Dance Clubs

Several music clubs and bars in Paris offer free entry, but expect high-priced drinks—up to 100F! To stay within our "extremely cheap" guidelines, order the cheapest item on the menu and nurse it all night.

Paris Sélection Loisirs

For 24-hour information about current Paris events and attractions, dial 49-52-53-56 for a taped message in English.

Television

If you don't feel like going out, watch French television for a unique entertainment experience. (If your room lacks a TV, the hotel lobby probably has one.) There are several channels—some run by the state, others privately owned—each with eclectic programming that is probably quite different from what you're used to. During prime-time, you'll find sitcoms, political commentaries, game shows, movies, and lots of short, 5-15 minute, vignette-style programs. It's fun to watch American programs (usually syndicated reruns) dubbed in French. The voices rarely match the original (imagine Bill Cosby with a very deep French voice).

Food & Dining

Baguette

It's one of the most common sights in Paris: someone walking down the street with a *baguette* in his hand. The long, slender stick of bread (*baguette* means "wand"), whose maximum price of 4.5F is set by the government, is one of the best bargains in the city. (The *demi-baguette* costs 2-4F.) The French, who consume more bread than anyone else in the world, often buy a *baguette* as a cheap afternoon snack.

Bars

Here's a great tip: if you consume food and drink standing at a bar, it's 50% cheaper than if you're served at a table.

Breakfast

To keep your costs down, avoid the costly breakfast (*petit déjeuner*) offered by your hotel. Instead, buy croissants (5F each on average) or other pastries at a nearby *boulangerie, patisserie,* or grocery, and, if you have room in your suitcase, bring a small coffee pot to make your morning brew. Breakfast served at a counter in a train station or department store and in uncelebrated cafés will be far less than at the hotel.

Cafés

Paris is known worldwide for its cafés. An outdoor seat along a busy street can be the best place in the whole city on a mild afternoon or summer night to people-watch and soak up the atmosphere. The coffee, food, and drinks are costly, but once you place an order, you can sit at a table for several hours if you please. Though the waiters will ask to refill your glass, you don't have to let them. Drink slowly, sit back, and enjoy. The most popular locations are **Aux Deux Magots** and **Café Flore** in the Quartier St-Germain-des-Prés, **Café Cluny** at the intersection of boulevards St-Germain and St-Michel, **Café Notre-Dame** at the corner of quai St-Michel and rue St-Jacques, and **La Coupole**, **La Rotonde**, and **Le Dôme** along boulevard Montparnasse.

Coffee

Coffee, usually served in a demitasse cup (request a *grande tasse* if you want a regular-sized cup), is one of the most expensive drinks in Paris. Although I usually avoid American establishments, McDonald's (known as *Le Petit Arch*) serves the cheapest coffee in Paris (5F). Otherwise, expect to pay 8-15F at stand-up counters, 10-35F in cafés.

Food Markets

Throughout Paris, several permanent food markets and others of a roving variety offer fresh food at inexpensive prices. A few notable markets are listed in the arrondissement chapters.

Lunch

To save money, plan picnic lunches in some of Paris's lovely parks. You can get ready-made sandwiches and other foods at many *charcuteries*, train stations, and grocery stores, or save even more by buying groceries and making your own lunch. A *baguette*, a small package of ham, cheese, potato chips, yogurt, and a two-liter bottle of mineral water will cost less than 25F. During the winter and on rainy days, you can take refuge in a train station waiting area. Officials rarely check for ticket hold-ers. Especially attractive parks are discussed in the arrondisse-ment chapters.

Supper

Dining in Paris restaurants will put a serious dent in your budg-et. A simple meal—a plain omelette or onion soup, green salad, and a half-liter bottle of mineral water—will cost about 60F. To reduce your costs, forsake appetizers, salads, desserts, and pricey drinks. (The tap water is safe to drink.) Many entrées come with a vegetable or a heaping portion of *pomme frites* (french fries) and a leafy garnish. Some restaurants offer an inexpensive, set price menu (*menu prix fixe*), where you get a complete meal (meat, vegetables, dessert, and drink) for one price. For information about types of Paris restaurants, see the *Paris Essentials* chapter.

Miscellaneous

Conferences/Expositions

As an international city, Paris hosts dozens of conferences and trade expositions every day (except holidays). Many are open to the public for free or extremely cheap admission. Check with the Office du Tourisme to see what conventions are in town.

Flowers

Everyday, the cemeteries of Paris throw away bushels of dried, semi-fresh, silk, and plastic flowers. If you see something you like in a trash can, it's free for the taking. If a caretaker objects, don't protest, and use discretion by not scattering the contents of the can all over the pavement. Never take anything off a gravestone, even if it looks decrepit.

Publications & Information

Office du Tourisme
The tourist information offices offer a wealth of free brochures, magazines, and maps upon request. See arrondissements 7, 8, 10, 12, 13, and 15 for addresses.

Miscellaneous Publications
There's a large assortment of free publications in Paris, ranging from simple brochures to slick, four-color magazines. Some of the best places to find these freebies are tourist offices, airline counters, hotels, book and music stores, markets, and some shop entrances. One of the best magazines is *The Free Voice*, a monthly produced by the Cooperative for Better Living in conjunction with the American Church (7th arrondissement). It has an interesting mix of articles (fiction and nonfiction), plus information about available jobs and current events. If you're looking for housing and/or a job in Paris, *France USA Contacts* is a good free source.

Pariscope
This cheap, 200-page magazine lists all the weekly entertainment, art expositions, conferences, sports, and other events occurring in Paris. Every issue also includes a listing of restaurants, museums, music clubs, parks, sports facilities, taxi stops, radio stations, and weekly television highlights. It costs 3F and hits the magazine kiosks every Wednesday.

L'Officiel des Spectacles
This magazine is similar to *Pariscope*. *L'Officiel des Spectacles* is better organized and only 2F, but it's not as comprehensive.

Recreation & Sports

Allo-Sports
For the latest sporting events information, call 42-72-54-54.

Boules

The classic game of *boules*, played in nearly every park and square with open space, is fun to watch, especially if it's a lively match. If your French is good and you know how to play (the closer your large metal ball is to the small ball, the more points you receive, plus you can knock your opponent's ball farther away—sort of like horseshoes), make an effort to join the fun.

Parks

There are over 400 parks in Paris, ranging from tiny, leafy squares in the middle of traffic intersections to the massive, multi-purpose Bois de Boulogne. The most popular and interesting parks are described in the arrondissement chapters.

Swimming Pools

After a hard day of touring, you might enjoy a relaxing swim in one of the city's well-maintained municipal pools (*municipale piscine*). Admission ranges from 10F-25F for a few hours of recreation. For more information and a complete list of pools in Paris, ask for the free brochure *Les Piscines à Paris* from the Hôtel de Ville, any arrondissement Mairie, or the Bureau des Sports (17 boulevard Morland, 4th arrondissement). *Pariscope* also lists a selection of pools with times and prices.

Shopping

Bouquinistes

On the sidewalks of the Seine River quais opposite the Ile de la Cité, you'll find the *bouquinistes*, vendors who sell used and antique books, magazines, comics, maps, prints, postcards, and other items, some at cheap prices, from the green padlocked boxes hooked onto the river parapets. They are found primarily on the Left Bank from quai de Conti to quai de Montebello and on the Right Bank from quai du Louvre to quai de Gesvres.

Flea Markets

For really cheap books, clothes, bric-a-brac, and other items, visit one of the city's flea markets. Some are well-organized in buildings and under tents; others are more impromptu. The best ones are listed in the arrondissement and suburb chapters.

Inno

Owned by MonoPrix (see below), this store offers good quality merchandise at discount prices, plus an excellent grocery store in the basement. On my last trip to Paris, I bought a terrific watch for only 175F. Its two Paris locations are 35 rue du Départ (across from the Gare Montparnasse) and 20 boulevard de Charonne in the 20th arrondissement.

Maps

Free maps of Paris, given away by the Office de Tourisme, large department stores, and hotels, make nice souvenirs, and we usually get extra copies to give to friends back home. Although they list only the main thoroughfares, they are colorfully illustrated with pictures of the city's primary sights and buildings.

MonoPrix / UniPrix / Prisunic

These stores, the French versions of Kmart, are excellent places to buy film, T-shirts, toiletries, and other items. Plus, each has a grocery, bakery, and lunch counter on the premises. There are several locations for each in Paris.

Postcards

The price of postcards at some of the major sights is ridiculously high. You can find the same (sometimes better) cards for 1-2F from the magazine kiosks on street corners.

Transportation

Buses (Public)

Over 2,000 buses crisscross Paris, and they're a great way to see the city cheaply, especially when you use a discount pass or tourist card for unlimited travel. Otherwise, each trip will cost 1-2 Métro tickets, depending on distance (more tickets if you take a suburban bus route [bus numbers 100 or higher]). For more information about the Paris bus system, see the *Paris Essentials* chapter. Some of the more scenic Paris bus routes with their highlights are as follows:

#21—Opéra, Palais Royal, Musée du Louvre, crosses Pont Neuf to follow Left Bank of Seine River to boulevard St-Michel, Jardin du Luxembourg, and Parc Montsouris.

#22—elegant 8th and 16th arrondissements, Arc de Triomphe, Grand Boulevards, Gare St-Lazare, and Opéra.

#24—place de la Concorde, Left Bank of the Seine River from Pont de la Concorde to Gare d'Austerlitz, Gare de Lyon, Omnisports complex, and Centre Culturel Americain. This is one of the longest bus routes in Paris.

#42—Opéra, place de la Concorde, up the avenue des Champs-Élysées briefly, Tour Eiffel, and Parc André Citröen.

#47—Forum des Halles, Cathédrale de Notre-Dame, and east side of 5th arrondissement.

#49—Grand Palais, Invalides, École Militaire, and UNESCO.

#52—Église de la Madeleine, rue Faubourg St-Honoré, Arc de Triomphe, and Bois de Boulogne.

#58—Jardin/Palais du Luxembourg, 6th arrondissement, Les Deux Magots café, Ile de la Cité, Pont Neuf, rue de Rivoli, and Hôtel de Ville.

#72—Right Bank of the Seine River from Porte de St-Cloud to Hôtel de Ville.

#73—Musée d'Orsay, place de la Concorde, avenue des Champs-Élysées, Arc de Triomphe, and La Défense.

#82—Palais des Congrés, Arc de Triomphe, Tour Eiffel, Invalides, Gare Montparnasse, and Jardin du Luxembourg.

#84—Panthéon, Jardin du Luxembourg, Église St-Sulpice, St-Germain-des Prés district, Musée d'Orsay, place de la Concorde, Église de la Madeleine, and Parc Monceau.

#87—place de la Bastille (new Opéra), east tip of Ile St-Louis, boulevard St-Germain through both the 5th and 6th arrondissements, École Militaire, and Tour Eiffel.

#95—St-Germain-des-Prés district, Pont Neuf, Musée du Louvre, Palais Royal, Opéra, and Cimetière Montmartre.

#96—boulevards St-Germain and St-Michel, Ile de la Cité,

Palais de Justice, Conciergerie, place du Châtelet, Hôtel de Ville, heart of the Marais district, and 20th arrondissement; another very long route.

Métro Carnet/Passes
When you purchase a *carnet* (ten tickets), you can ride the Métro for as little as 4.6F per ticket (single price is 8F). The weekly and monthly passes for unlimited travel reduce costs considerably, even if you only take two trips per day. There are passes for all eight RER travel zones. For more Métro information, see the *Paris Essentials* chapter.

Scenic Métro Lines
Another cheap way to tour Paris is to ride the open-air Métro lines (ground level, elevated railways, and in open channels). The lines offer these sights:

Métro line 1—The south platform of this line at the place de la Bastille station overlooks the Port de Plaisance de Paris-Arsenal.

Métro line 2—This subway follows the 10th and 18th arrondissement border on an elevated railway from the Barbès Rochechouart station to the place du Colonel-Fabien station. There are views of the Gare du Nord, Gare du l'Est, Rotonde de la Villette, and Canal St-Martin.

Métro line 5—This train travels from the St-Marcel station on an elevated railway for a short distance to the Gare d'Austerlitz station, then crosses the Seine River to the quai de la Rapée station.

Métro line 6—From the Passy station, this subway crosses the Seine River, offers good views of the Tour Eiffel, then travels for a long distance on an elevated railway through the 15th arrondissement to the Pasteur station, where it goes underground. It comes above ground again at the St-Jacques station. From there, it travels through the 13th arrondissement on an elevated railway, except for a few short tunnels to the Seine River, which it crosses to the Bercy station.

RER line B—From the Denfert-Rochereau station, this train travels on an elevated railway to Parc Montsouris, then through the park in an open channel to the Cité Universitaire station.

RER line C—From the Champ de Mars/Tour Eiffel station, this line travels briefly along the Seine River, then crosses it (C-1, 3) to the Maison de Radio-France station. Another section of the line (C-5, 7) continues south along the river into the suburbs.

1st Arrondissement

The small 1st arrondissement is the heart of Paris's history and the home to some of its best museums and monuments. You will find the Ile de la Cité, Musée du Louvre, Sainte-Chapelle, Palais Royal, and Jardin des Tuileries—plus one of Paris's most popular shopping areas, with the subterranean Forum les Halles shopping mall, Samaritaine department store, luxury furnishings at place Vendôme, and a variety of shops catering to tourists along the rue de Rivoli.

The boundaries of the 1st arrondissement are rues des Petits-Champs and Étienne-Marcel (north), Seine River and west side of Ile de la Cité (south), boulevards du Palais and de Sébastopol (east), and place de la Concorde and rue St-Florentin (west).

Ile de la Cité

Though the largest of the two islands in the center of the city lacks the medieval character it had before Baron Haussmann's workers tore down much of the quarter and widened the streets, the Ile de la Cité remains one of the city's most historic areas. Its primary sights are the stained glass windows of Sainte-Chapelle (see below) and the Cathédrale de Notre-Dame (see 4th arrondissement). Walk both banks of the Seine River to get a good look at it. *Address:* center of Paris, in the Seine River. *Métro/Buses:* See sights below. **Note:** Some of the buses listed for the Ile de la Cité sights do not travel on the island but have stops on the river quais across from it.

Square du Vert Galant

At the western tip of the Ile de la Cité, there's a sedate park framed by chestnut and willow trees hanging over its pathways. It's a relaxing place to watch the Seine River boat traffic on a pretty day. *Address:* off place du Pont Neuf. To reach it, descend the steps behind the Henri IV equestrian monument to a small

park, following the paths to the river. *Métro:* Pont Neuf (7).
Buses: 21, 24, 27, 58, 67, 69, 70, 72, 74, 75, 76, 81, 85.

Place Dauphine

Opposite the Henri IV monument is one of the most peaceful
residential areas in Paris. With a triangular-shaped park at its
center, place Dauphine is flanked on two sides by slender town
houses with uniform façades and the rear of the Palais de Justice
on its east end. At street level, the buildings contain one of the
cheapest hotels in Paris, a tea salon, restaurants, a wine bar, and
other shops. *Address:* between buildings off place du Pont
Neuf. Métro/*Buses:* same as Square du Vert Galant.

Pont Neuf

The "New" Bridge is now the oldest bridge in Paris.
Constructed from 1578-1604, it was the first built in Paris with
pedestrian sidewalks instead of houses lining its sides. Duck
into one of its half-circle portals with stone seats to rest or get a
view of the Seine River, and don't miss the stone carvings on its
exterior. In September 1985, the controversial artist Christo
wrapped the entire bridge and its lamps in brown gauze. *Address:* connects quai du Louvre (Right Bank) across western tip
of the Ile de la Cité to quai de Conti (Left Bank). *Métro/Buses:*
same as Square du Vert Galant.

Samaritaine

This is the department store where working-class Parisians
shop. You can buy the inexpensive blue pants and shirts the
street workers wear, chef's toque, and the same signs used in
buildings and hotels. Its prices for souvenirs are cheaper than at
other Paris department stores. The best part of this old store
(built in 1903 in the art nouveau style, with lots of decorative
glass and steel) is its 360-degree rooftop (free admission) view
over Paris, especially of the Ile de la Cité and Seine River. To get
there, take the elevator to the ninth floor in Building 2, then
walk up one flight of stairs to the 10th floor, where there's a café
and rooftop terrace. But, before you settle for this level, look for
a narrow staircase that leads you even higher. Attached to the
railing of this small round perch are colored metal sketches
describing the sights in the distance. For close-up views, try the
coin-operated telescopes. *Address:* corner of quai du Louvre
and rue de la Monnaie opposite the Pont Neuf (phone 40-41-

20-20). *Hours:* Mon, Wed, Sat 9:30am-6:30pm; Tue, Thur, Fri 9:30am-8:30pm. Café/terrace closed Oct 1-March 31 and Sundays. *Métro/Buses:* same as Square du Vert Galant.

Conciergerie

Resembling a fortress, this former medieval palace gained its greatest notoriety as a prison and final home for those who awaited execution by guillotine during the French Revolution's Reign of Terror. The cell of Marie Antoinette is here, plus, for free, take a look at its massive 14th-century public clock decorated with *fleur-de-lis,* angels, and royal shields. It's mounted on the tower at the corner of quai de l'Horloge and boulevard du Palais. *Address:* 1 quai de l'Horloge on the Ile de la Cité (phone 43-54-30-06). *Hours:* June 1-Aug 31: daily 9:30am-6:30pm; Sept 1-30, April 1-May 31: 10am-5pm; Oct 1-March 31: 10am-4:30pm. *Métro:* Cité (4). *Buses:* 21, 24, 27, 38, 47, 58, 69, 70, 72, 74, 81, 85, 96. *Admission:* Carte Musées et Monuments.

Palais de Justice

Royal and administrative buildings have occupied this site, starting with the Palace of Roman Governors, later the residence of Merovingian and Capetian kings. After the last king departed in 1358, the building became a court of law and was the site of many death sentences during the Reign of Terror. The current building was constructed by Baron Haussmann in 1860. You can wander through its halls or attend a courtroom session, though it will help if you understand some French. *Address:* 2 boulevard du Palais on the Ile de la Cité (phone 43-29-12-55). *Hours:* Mon-Fri 9am-5pm. *Métro/Buses:* same as Conciergerie.

Sainte-Chapelle

The narrow Sainte-Chapelle, located in the courtyard between the Palais de Justice and Conciergerie, is considered the finest example of Gothic architecture in Paris. Constructed in 1241 to house the holy relics (including the purported crown of Christ, two sections of his cross with a nail from it, and the Roman soldier's lance that pierced Christ's side) acquired at Constantinople by the Crusaders, the building features 15 original stained glass windows in its upper chapel and other amazing feats of artistic craftsmanship. On a few Sundays during the summer, it hosts free concerts. *Address:* 4 boulevard du Palais (phone 43-54-30-09). *Hours:* 10am-5pm; closed Jan 1, May 1,

Nov 1, Nov 11, Dec 25. *Métro/Buses:* same as Conciergerie. *Admission:* Carte Musées et Monuments.

Marché aux Fleurs & Marché aux Oiseaux

The bustling flower market situated between the Cité Métro station entrance and Seine River is great fun to browse. You may smell and look at the flowers, but don't touch unless you intend to buy. On Sundays, this area becomes a bird market with a variety of winged creatures for sale. *Address:* place Louis Lépine on the Ile de la Cité. *Hours:* daily 8am-7:30pm. *Métro/Buses:* same as Conciergerie.

Église St-Germain-l'Auxerrois

Often overlooked by tourists heading for the Musée du Louvre across the street, the Église St-Germain-l'Auxerrois is an excellent example of the Flamboyant Gothic architectural style. It was also the house of worship for the royal family before the French Revolution. Built during the 13th-16th centuries, it features numerous statues in wood and stone, several paintings from the period, and *La Marie,* the bell rung after the St-Bartholomew's Eve massacre (August 24, 1572) of over 3,000 French Huguenots. Many artists and architects of the court, including Boucher, Nattier, Chardin, Van Loo, and Le Vau, are buried here. *Address:* place du Louvre. *Métro:* Louvre-Rivoli (1). *Buses:* 21, 67, 68, 69, 72, 74, 76, 81, 85, 95.

Musée du Louvre

The Musée du Louvre, housed in the largest royal palace in Europe, is a mind-boggling collection of over 300,000 pieces of art, plus the Crown Jewels and various antique collections. With four floors of almost unending art galleries and hallways that seem to run for miles, the Louvre is impossible to tour in one day. At the entrance, get a map and head for the highlights like the *Mona Lisa,* the *Venus de Milo,* the huge David paintings, and other favorites you may have. When you tire from gawking at the art, consider the building's finely painted, gilded ceilings and walls—some of the finest decorative craftsmanship found anywhere.

If you hate long lines, don't go to the glass pyramid created by I.M. Pei in the former palace courtyard, which serves as the main entrance. Instead, enter at *Porte Jaujard* (at the far end of the Musée du Louvre, at the Tuileries and Seine River corner),

The main entrance of the Musée du Louvre is a controversial glass pyramid designed by I.M. Pei. (photo: Rollin Riggs)

where you'll rarely wait.

A few years ago as part of the "Grand Louvre" project, an underground shopping mall opened with 60 boutiques, an auditorium for fashion shows, and four large meeting rooms, all connected by a shop-lined tunnel to the lobby beneath the pyramid.

Address: main entrance at cour Napoléon. Entire complex bounded by rue de Rivoli (north), Seine River (south), rue de l'Amiral de Coligny (east), and avenue du Géneral Lemonnier (west) (phone 40-20-51-51 for answering machine in English and French). *Hours:* Thur-Sun 9am-6pm; Mon & Wed 9am-9:45pm (Sully and Denon wings open alternate weeknights; lobby open until 10pm). *Métro:* Palais Royal-Musée du Louvre (1, 7), Louvre-Rivoli (1). *Buses:* 21, 24, 27, 39, 48, 67, 69, 72, 74, 76, 77, 81, 85, 95. *Admission:* Free the first Sunday of each month; 26F after 3pm and all day Sunday (a bargain, since you'll probably spend all day there), Carte Musées et Monuments. Free entry through the pyramid into underground lobby with bookstores and gift shops.

Musée des Arts Décoratifs & Musée de l'Affiche et de la Publicité

The city's main decorative arts museum, housed in the Pavillon de Marsan wing of the Musée du Louvre, features over 100,000 items from the Middle Ages to the present, including furniture, tapestries, porcelain, and paintings by Cranach, David, Ingres, and Dubuffet. The second museum documents the history of posters and other advertising materials. *Address:* 107 rue de Rivoli (phone 42-60-32-14). *Hours:* Wed-Sat 12:30pm-6:30pm, Sun 11am-6pm. *Métro:* Palais Royal-Musée du Louvre (1, 7), Tuileries (1). *Buses:* 21, 27, 39, 48, 68, 72, 81, 95. *Admission:* Carte Musées et Monuments.

Arc de Triomphe du Carrousel

Between the Jardin des Tuileries and Musée de Louvre, a miniature version of the Arc de Triomphe was erected in 1806 under the order of Napoléon to honor his soldiers and to be used as a new entrance to the Tuileries Palace (destroyed by the 1871 Commune). Today, it overlooks the triumphs of modern architecture, as the Louvre continues to change above and below ground. Based on the triumphal arch of Roman Emperor Septimus Severus (203 AD), the Arc is decorated with a goddess of peace in a chariot and bas-relief scenes that illustrate Napoleon's German and Austrian campaigns. *Address:* avenue du General Lemonnier. *Métro:* Palais Royal-Musée du Louvre (1, 7), Tuileries (1). *Buses:* 27, 39, 48, 81, 95.

Jardin des Tuileries

For one of the best promenades in Paris, walk down the middle of the Jardin des Tuileries. You get a gorgeous, clear sight line up the avenue des Champs-Élysées to the Arc de Triomphe. Laid out in the 1560's between the Louvre and place de la Concorde, the former formal garden of the Tuileries Palace is a favorite of Parisians and tourists alike, who come to admire its large fountains at both ends, sweeping flower displays at the place de la Concorde gate, and hundreds of statues. The elevated terrace at the south end has good views of the Seine River and Musée d'Orsay. *Address:* enter off rue de Rivoli (north), quai des Tuileries (south), avenue du General Lemonnier (east), or place de la Concorde (west). *Hours:* Oct 1-March 31: daily 7am-8pm; April 1-Sept 30: 7am-10pm. *Métro:* Concorde (1, 8, 12), Tuileries (1). *Buses:* 24, 42, 52, 68, 69, 72, 73, 84, 94.

Musée de l'Orangerie
The basement of this art museum contains the *Grandes Nympheas*, a series of large water lily paintings by Claude Monet, done during his final years at Giverny. The museum also features important paintings by Rousseau, Cézanne, Renoir, Matisse, Picasso, and Modigliani. *Address:* southwest corner of Jardin des Tuileries (phone 42-97-48-16). *Hours:* Wed-Mon 9:45am-5pm; closed Jan 1, May 1, Dec 25. *Métro/Buses:* same as Jardin des Tuileries. *Admission:* Carte Musées et Monuments.

Comédie Française
Annexed to the southwest corner of the Palais Royal, the 1790 building of Comédie Française has been the national theater since 1792. All shows are in French. *Address:* place André-Malraux, next to the Palais Royal (phone 40-15-00-15). *Métro/Buses:* same as Jardin du Palais Royal. *Admission:* 30F for tickets not claimed or sold 45 minutes before curtain. Get in line an hour or two before show time.

Espace Japan
The Japanese cultural center has exhibitions of contemporary art, design, and graphics. *Address:* 12 rue Ste-Anne (phone 42-61-60-83). *Hours:* Mon-Sat 10am-6pm. *Métro:* Pyramides (7). *Buses:* 39, 68, 81, 95.

Jardin du Palais Royal
Since it can't be seen from the street, tourists often miss this beautiful park, annexed to the palace built for Cardinal Richelieu in the 1630's. Surrounded by an arcaded building with elegant apartments and government offices, the Jardin is a quiet and romantic spot, with tree-lined paths, fountains, flowers, and benches. It's simply one of the best free sights in Paris.

Beneath the arcades, you'll find interesting boutiques and the

The 260 striped columns of varying lengths, found in the former courtyard of the Palais Royal, is one of the oddest art installations in the world. Tourists, children, and dogs appreciate it best.

three-star restaurant **Le Grand Véfour**, frequented by Napoléon and Josephine, Victor Hugo, Collette, and other celebrities since the 1760's. Also, don't miss the modern chrome ball fountain and the odd sight of 260 striped columns filling the former palace courtyard, still a controversial art installation enjoyed mainly by children, tourists, and dogs. *Address:* place du Palais Royal. *Métro:* Palais Royal-Musée du Louvre (1, 7). *Buses:* 21, 27, 29, 39, 48, 67, 69, 72, 74, 81, 85, 95.

Les Louvre des Antiquaires

Across from the Musée du Louvre and adjacent to the Palais Royal, this former department store is packed with 250 art galleries and antique shops. It's a great place for browsing and an extremely cheap introduction to European and decorative furnishings, especially if you don't visit the Musée des Arts Decoratifs. *Address:* 2 place du Palais Royal (phone 42-97-27-00) *Hours:* Tue-Sun 11am-7pm. *Métro/Buses:* same as Jardin du Palais Royal.

Rue de Rivoli

A shop on this arcaded street, one of the longest in Paris, can be a gold mine for a Parisian vendor. Traveling east from the place de la Concorde to its end in the Marais district (where its name changes to the rue St-Antoine), rue de Rivoli sees a constant flood of tourists going to the Louvre and other sights near it. If your time is short in Paris and you want a souvenir, plenty of shops here will help you, some with bargain prices. But exercise caution—it's prime territory for pickpockets and other con artists. *Métro:* Concorde (1, 8, 12), Tuileries (1), Palais Royal-Musée du Louvre (1, 7), Louvre-Rivoli (1), Châtelet (1, 4, 7, 11), Hôtel de Ville (1, 11), St-Paul (1). *Buses:* 21, 67, 68, 69, 72, 74, 75, 76, 81, 85, 96, plus any of the buses going to the sights near this street.

Galerie Véro-Dodat

The block-long Galerie Véro-Dodat is considered the loveliest of the restored 19th-century *passages* (narrow, covered shopping streets built through buildings—precursors of the shopping mall) in Paris. With painted ceilings, gas lights, and paneled store fronts divided by black marble columns, the Galerie features interesting stores and a *salon de thé*. *Address:* enter off rue Croix des Petits-Champs or rue J.J. Rousseau. *Métro:* Palais Royal-Musée du Louvre (1, 7). *Buses:* 21, 27, 39, 48, 67, 74, 85, 95.

Temple de l'Oratoire

Formerly owned by the *Congrégation de l'Oratoire de France* (a fraternity devoted to religious instruction and the art of preaching), this small church built in 1616 features a large monument on its south façade dedicated to Admiral Gaspard de Coligny (1517-72), the leader of the French Huguenots, who was murdered on St. Bartholomew's Eve. *Address:* rue St-Honoré at rue de l'Oratoire. *Métro:* Louvre-Rivoli (1). *Buses:* 21, 67, 69, 74.

Joan of Arc Monument

A gilded statue of the "Maid of Orleans" atop her horse watches tourists on rue de Rivoli opposite the entrance to the Musée des Arts Decoratifs. On this site in 1429, Joan tried to penetrate the English line and liberate Paris. Instead, she caught an arrow in her thigh, causing her and the French army to withdraw from the city. Two years later, she was burned at the stake in Rouen for heresy against the Catholic church. *Address:* place des Pyramides. *Métro:* Tuileries (1). *Buses:* 21, 27, 29, 68, 81, 95.

W. H. Smith

This bookstore, featuring the largest selection of English-language books and magazines in Paris, is an oasis for tourists in search of reading material—and other English-speaking people. Browsing is free, and they usually have a good selection of free magazines and brochures at the entrance. *Address:* 248 rue de Rivoli (phone 42-60-37-97). *Hours:* Mon-Sat 9:30am-7pm. *Métro:* Concorde (1, 8, 12). *Buses:* 24, 42, 52, 72, 73, 84, 94.

Église St-Roch

Tucked into a narrow city block is a historic Baroque-designed church (built in 1730), where Napoléon's forces clashed with Royalist troops in 1795. The pock marks in its façade are from bullets fired during a skirmish on the steps. Inside, the church has an interesting altarpiece, semicircular apse, numerous statues, sculpture, paintings, beautiful ceilings, and circa-1752 rococo organ. It also contains the tombs of several famous Frenchmen, including the poet Corneille, philosopher Diderot, and garden designer Le Nôtre. Free recitals and classical music concerts are held here every week. *Address:* rue St-Honoré at rue St-Roch. *Métro:* Tuileries (1). *Buses:* 68, 72.

Place Vendôme

At the center of this semi-enclosed square dominated by the Hôtel Ritz, Cartier jewelry shop, and other posh boutiques, the 144-foot **Colonne de la Grande Armée** features a statue of Napoléon dressed as Julius Caesar and spiraling sheets of bronze carved with scenes from the Napoleonic Wars. During the 1871 Commune uprising, the column was torn down and broken into several pieces. *Address:* crossed north-south by rue de la Paix/rue de Castiglione. *Métro:* Tuileries (1). *Buses:* 29, 72.

Hôtel Ritz

In business since 1705, the luxurious Hôtel Ritz is the bastion of the rich and famous. The only way to see its interior is to have a reason to be there—meeting someone at its restaurant, tea room, etc. Otherwise, the doorman will spin you back outside through the revolving door. Try to look rich and important, and come up with a good excuse! *Address:* 15 place Vendôme. *Hours:* early morning-midnight. *Métro/Buses:* same as place Vendôme.

Place des Victoires

Surrounding this traffic circle designed by Mansart in 1685 (with a great equestrian statue of Louis XIV at its center), the shops of major fashion designers—including Kenzo, Thiery Mugler, and Jean-Paul Gaultier—are open to fashionable browsers. *Address:* crossed east-west by rue Étienne-Marcel/rue des Petits-Champs. (The north half of the circle is in the 2nd arrondissement.) *Métro:* Sentier (8). *Buses:* 29, 48.

Bourse du Commerce

Next to the south side of the circular Commercial Exchange (accredited brokers only) with its iron and glass dome, you'll see a 101-foot, fluted column topped by a giant iron cage—the only remains of the Hôtel de la Reine, a mansion built in 1572 for Catherine de Medici. The column was used by her astrologer for stargazing. *Address:* rue de Viarmes. *Métro:* Louvre-Rivoli (1), Les Halles (4). *Buses:* 48, 67, 74, 85.

Forum des Halles

On the site of the former central food market of Paris, this unique, ultra-modern, multi-level shopping mall boasts movie theaters, restaurants, a swimming pool, over 200 stores, and a few pricey museums. It's a popular meeting spot for Parisian youth and—beware—pickpockets. Between the Forum and the Bourse La Commerce, the **Jardin des Halles** has meandering paths and Brancusi's giant sculpture of a head held in a hand (near the rear of the Église St-Eustache—see below). Beneath the complex and park is the city's largest Métro station, Châtelet/Les Halles, which has connections to the separate Les

Halles and Châtelet stations. *Address:* rue Pierre Lescot at rue Berger. *Hours:* Mon-Sat 9am-8pm for most shops, later hours on weekends and for movie theaters, restaurants, and entertainment facilities. *Métro:* Châtelet/Les Halles (A, B, D), Châtelet (1, 4, 7, 11), Les Halles (4). *Buses:* 21, 29, 38, 47, 67, 74, 75, 85.

Vidéothèque de Paris

Considering the high price of movies in Paris, this is a great bargain. For 30F, you can watch four videos or movies screened each day in the projection room. Plus, in the *Salle Pierre,* you can choose your own selection from over 4,000 film clips, newsreels, commercials, documentaries, soap operas, and other clips about Paris from 1896 to the present. In a laboratory-like atmosphere, you get your own cubicle and screen, and instructions are available in English. *Address:* 2 Grande Galerie (Port St-Eustache entrance in Forum des Halles) (phone 40-26-34-30). *Hours:* Tue-Sun 12:30pm-8:30pm. *Métro/Buses:* same as Forum des Halles. *Admission:* 22F.

Espace Photographique de Paris

Financed by the city, this gallery features temporary exhibitions of famous international photographers. *Address:* 4-8 Grande Galerie (Niveau 1-Porte Pont Neuf in the Forum des Halles) (phone 42-86-87-12). *Hours:* Tue-Sun 1pm-6pm. *Métro/Buses:* same as Forum des Halles.

FNAC Photo Gallery

FNAC is a discount chain selling books, cassettes, CD's, cameras, film, concert tickets, and other entertainment products. At this location and its other large stores at 136 rue de Rennes (6th arrondissement) and 26 avenue de Wagram (8th arrondissement), it has a photo gallery featuring work by local photographers and occasional exhibitions by renowned contemporary photographers. Free concerts are sometimes held in the stores. *Address:* Level 3 in the Forum des Halles (phone 42-86-87-12). *Hours:* Mon 1pm-7:30pm, Tue-Sat 10am-7:30pm. *Métro/Buses:* same as Forum des Halles.

Musée Pierre Marly-Lunettes et Lorgnettes de Jadis

This optician's shop displays a collection of 3,000 unique items of eyewear, including spectacles, *pince-nez,* opera glasses, and binoculars from the 13th century to the present day. *Address:*

380 rue St-Honore (phone 40-20-06-98). *Hours:* Tue-Sat 10am-noon & 2pm-6pm; closed August. *Métro:* Concorde (1, 8, 12). *Buses:* 24. *Admission:* 20F.

Église St-Eustache
The huge Église St-Eustache, set on a small square just west of the Forum des Halles, is the Right Bank's answer to the Cathédrale de Notre-Dame. Built from 1532 to 1637 and modified over the centuries, its architecture ranges from Gothic to Classical, with flying buttresses, sculpture, outstanding stained glass windows (dating from 1631), large bell towers, the tomb of Colbert (Finance Minister under King Louis XIV), numerous paintings (including a Rubens), frescos, and other art and craftsmanship from the period. Famous for the lovely tone of its 19th-century organ, the church hosted Berlioz in 1855 and Liszt in 1866. Today, occasional free classical music concerts are held here. *Address:* rue du Jour (main entrance). *Métro:* Les Halles (4). *Buses:* 29, 67, 74, 75, 85.

Fontaine des Innocents
This magnificent fountain, looking like a miniature temple with cascading water sliding down several levels, is set in an open square adjacent to Forum des Halles. Built in 1547, it's an excellent example of early-Renaissance architecture. Constructed over a cemetery (whose skeletons and bones were transferred to the Catacombes—see 14th arrondissement—in 1786), the fountain has become a favorite gathering place for Parisian youth. *Address:* rue Berger. *Métro:* Châtelet (1, 4, 7, 11), Châtelet/Les Halles (A, B, D). *Buses:* same as Forum des Halles.

Église St-Leu-St-Gilles
Located near the convergence of arrondissements 1 and 4, this is one of the oldest churches in Paris. The foundation was dedicated in 1235 to the Provençal hermit St-Gilles, and the church has been remodeled several times over the centuries since construction began in 1320. Admire the Neo-Gothic accents on its front façade and go inside to see the ancient nave and circa-1611 choir. *Address:* 92 rue St-Denis. *Métro:* Étienne-Marcel (4). *Buses:* 29, 38.

2nd Arrondissement

The 2nd arrondissement is one of Paris's oldest business districts. While not abundant in tourist sights, it does offer a good look at working Paris. Of interest to tourists are the Bourse (stock exchange), Bibliothèque Nationale, and several 19th-century *passages* in the area. Avoid the east end, intersected by the north-south rue St-Denis, at night—it's a seedy area frequented by prostitutes and low-lifes.

The 2nd arrondissement's boundaries are boulevards Montmartre, Poissonnière, Bonne Nouvelle, and St-Denis (north), rues des Petits-Champs and Étienne-Marcel (south), boulevard de Sébastopol (east), and boulevards des Capucines and des Italiens (west).

Galerie Colbert & Galerie Vivienne

A few steps north of the Palais Royal, two interconnecting *passages* have been restored to their 19th-century splendor. The Galerie Colbert, with its beautiful glass-domed ceiling and faux marble columns, is used primarily for offices and galleries (some are free) of the Bibliothèque Nationale (see below). That organization's auditorium in this passage offers a number of free lectures and debates throughout the year. (A schedule of events is available at the entrance.)

The Galerie Vivienne, with a tiled mosaic walkway and bas-reliefs on the wall, features shops selling books, cards, gadgets, and fabric, plus there's a Jean-Paul Gaultier clothing boutique, a wine merchant, and a salon de thé. *Address:* enter at 6 rue des Petit-Champs or 2 rue Vivienne. *Métro:* Bourse (3), Palais Royal-Musée du Louvre (1, 7). *Buses:* 29, 39, 48, 67, 74, 95.

Musée-Vitrines des Arts du Spectacle

The museum of entertainment arts, under the auspices of the Bibliothèque Nationale's Départment des Arts du Spectacles, offers several temporary exhibitions each year. *Address:* Passage Colbert (phone 42-77-44-21). *Hours:* Mon-Sat 8am-6pm. *Métro/Buses:* same as Galerie Vivienne/Galerie Colbert. *Admission:* varies from free to 20F, depending on the exhibition.

Bibliothèque Nationale

Since 1537, every book printed in the country has been sent to this building, the national library of France. Its collection, housed in two 17th-century mansions with a beautiful reading room built in 1864 over the Mazarin courtyard (featuring nine square vaulted bays supported by cast-iron columns and arches), includes over 12 million books and engravings, over 130,000 original manuscripts, many original drawings, two Gutenberg Bibles, and maps dating from the 13th century. Several exhibitions on the history of books are hosted here every year. *Address:* main entrance at 58 rue de Richelieu; courtyard with fountain off rue Vivienne (phone 47-03-83-30). *Hours:* Mon-Sat 10am-8pm for galleries. *Métro/Buses:* same as Galerie Vivienne/Galerie Colbert. *Admission:* You can peek into the reading room, but you can't go into the book stacks without permission.

Cabinet des Médailles

A minor portion of the Bibliothèque Nationale's collection of coins, medals, cameos, swords, and other antiques discovered in France is shown in this gallery. *Address:* mezzanine level in Bibliothèque Nationale. *Hours:* 1pm-5pm, holidays noon-6pm. *Métro/Buses:* same as Bibliothèque Nationale. *Admission:* 22F (12F on Sunday).

Phonothèque Nationale

The small annex across the street contains the Bibliothèque Nationale's music library, with 400,000 records and 16,000 tapes, plus its collection of two million photographs. A photo gallery offers several temporary exhibitions each year focusing on a specific theme or photographer. *Address:* 4 rue de Louvois. *Hours:* Mon-Fri 1pm-5pm. *Métro:* Bourse (3), Quatre de Septembre (3). *Buses:* 29, 39, 48, 74. *Admission:* photo gallery free; you must be a member of the Bibliothèque Nationale to listen to recordings.

Passage Choiseul

One of the oldest *passages* in Paris is on the west side of the arrondissement. Built in 1825 with a skylight, it features Ionic columns and arches along storefronts selling art, clothes, shoes, toys, and other products. There's also an excellent *salon de thé* here. *Address:* enter at 40 rue des Petits-Champs or 23 rue St-Augustin. *Métro:* Quatre de Septembre (3), Pyramides (7). *Buses:* 29, 39.

Passage des Panoramas, Jouffry, & Verdeau Galeries des Varieties, St-Marc, & Montmartre

Except for crossing two streets, these *passages* are the longest group (approximately six blocks) of interconnecting *passages* in Paris. They contain a variety of shops (some over 100 years old, passed down through families) selling antiques, books, cameras, puppets and toys, Asian exports, luggage, gifts, and much more. You'll also find a food market, bars, restaurants, a thrift store, the two-star Hôtel Chopin, an engraver, and a printing shop. The *passages* Jouffry and Verdeau, which have more interesting shops plus a side entrance to the pricey Musée Grévin (a wax museum for 48F), are in the 9th arrondissement. The *passage* des Panoramas, open since 1800, is the oldest of the group. *Address:* enter off rues St-Marc, Montmartre, de la Grange Batelière, du Faubourg-Montmartre, or boulevard Montmartre. *Métro:* Le Peletier (7), Rue Montmartre (8, 9), Bourse (3). *Buses:* 20, 39, 48, 67, 74, 85.

Rue St-Denis

The narrow rue St-Denis, still the main pilgrimage road to St-Denis (where the Kings of France are buried), cuts through the heart of Paris's garment district, north of the Forum des Halles. See it during the day when it's full of activity, as workers push clothes down the street—but avoid it at night, since it's prime turf for prostitutes, drug dealers, and other shady characters. *Address:* from rue Étienne-Marcel to Porte St-Denis. *Métro:* Étienne-Marcel (4), Réaumur Sébastopol (3, 4), Strasbourg/St-Denis (4, 8, 9). *Buses:* 20, 29, 38, 39, 47.

Basilique Notre-Dame-des-Victoires

In 1629, King Louis XIII personally laid the foundation stone for this Augustinian church, whose members wanted to commemorate the downfall of the Protestants at La Rochelle in 1627.

Passage des Panoramas

Austere on the outside, the church's interior features a high altar with a gilded bronze relief of Christ's entombment and Van Loo paintings depicting St. Augustine's life. Another painting above the altar shows the King and Cardinal Richelieu committing themselves into the hands of the Mother of God before the battle of La Rochelle. The stained glass window above the altar continues the theme of God and King. The church also contains the tomb of Lully, court composer to King Louis XIV. *Address:* place des Petits Pères. *Métro:* Bourse (3). *Buses:* 20, 29, 48.

Passage du Caire & Galeries St-Caire, St-Denis, Ste-Foy

Toward the north end of rue St-Denis, a series of interconnecting *passages* are occupied by wholesale clothes businesses. The *passage* du Caire, with its pseudo-Egyptian arches, is the oldest *passage* (1799) in this district. *Address:* enter off rues St-Denis, Ste-Foy, or du Caire. *Métro:* Réaumur Sébastopol (3, 4), Strasbourg/St-Denis (4, 8, 9). *Buses:* 20, 38, 39, 47.

Passage du Grand-Cerf

After years of neglect and occupancy by textile companies, this renovated, three-story *passage* has returned to its 19th-century purpose by being rented to merchants selling consumer products. Built in 1825 with a checkered tile floor and magnificent glass skylight, it's the largest *passage* in Paris. *Address:* enter off rue St-Denis or rue Dussoubs. *Métro:* Étienne-Marcel (4). *Buses:* 29, 47.

3rd Arrondissement

The small, irregularly-shaped 3rd arrondissement is divided between a working-class district on the north and the Marais area, a former marsh where wealthy 17th-century Parisians built elegant mansions known as *Hôtel Particuliers*. Today, the Marais is again a fashionable area to live, as many of the *nouveau riche* have bought property there, and several area mansions display the collections of some of the city's finest museums.

The boundaries of the 3rd arrondissement are boulevards St-Denis, St-Martin, and place de la République (north), rues Rambuteau and des Francs-Bourgeois (south), boulevards du Temple, des Filles du Calvaire, and Beaumarchais (east), and boulevard de Sébastopol (west).

Musée des Arts et Metiers-Techniques

This interesting museum displays over 80,000 items illustrating science and industry from the 16th to 20th century. The collection includes historic clocks, Pascal's calculating machines, weaving machines, printing presses, early cameras, automobiles, astronomical instruments, and at least one representative of every type of machine made during this time span. One of the museum's galleries is housed in the 11th-century Église St-Martin-des-Champs, a church belonging to the once-powerful abbey at Cluny. *Address:* 292 rue St-Martin (phone 40-27-23-31). *Hours:* Tue-Sun 10am-5:30pm. *Métro:* Arts et Metiers (3, 11), Réaumur-Sébastopol (3, 4). *Buses:* 27, 38, 47, 75.

Église St-Nicolas-des-Champs

A half-block south of the Musée des Techniques, this church shows the contrast between Gothic and Renaissance architecture. It features a large Gothic tower built from 1420-80, a two-tiered altar topped by four angels with a massive candelabrum, and numerous paintings. Its 17th-century organ is one of the best in Paris, and there are frequent free concerts. *Address:* 252 rue St-Martin. *Métro/Buses:* same as Musée des Techniques.

Quartier de l'Horloge

This modern and jumbled area, located directly north of the Centre Georges Pompidou, is a mix of good and awful urban planning. Thrust into the middle of an Old World quarter, some of the structures fit well, while others never should have been built. Its best feature is the mechanical clock on rue Bernard-de-Clairvaux, where St. George defends time against a dragon, bird, or crab on the hour. (At noon, 6pm, and 10pm, all three creatures attack at the same time.) For a midnight snack, shop at **As Eco**, the largest supermarket in Paris (open until 1am). It's in the Horloge quarter at 11 rue Brantôme. *Address:* approximate boundaries are rue du Grenier St-Lazare (north), rue Rambuteau (south), rue Beaubourg (east), & rue St-Martin (west). *Métro:* Rambuteau (11). *Buses:* 29, 47.

Square du Temple

In the 12th century, the neighborhood surrounding this pretty square was the domain of the Knights Templar, a religious and military order founded in 1118. A popular organization with power that rivaled the Crown, it was dissolved in Paris in 1307 when its leaders were executed and its property was divided between the Crown and the Knights of St. John of Malta. During the French Revolution, the Knights' fortress on the square became a prison and was the first stop for King Louis XIV and the royal family after their arrest. Louis stayed there until his execution by guillotine on January 21, 1793. Napoléon had the prison torn down in 1808 to prevent Royalist pilgrimages to the site. *Address:* bordered by rue Perrée (north), rue de Bretagne (south), rue Eugène Spuller (east), and rue du Temple (west). *Métro:* Temple (3). *Buses:* 20, 75.

Marché du Temple

Opposite the Square du Temple on an entire block, a covered market sells new clothes at wholesale prices. If you are willing to dig, you'll find good merchandise at extremely cheap prices. *Address:* Carreau du Temple building. Enter off rue Dupetit Thouars (north), rue Perrée (south), rue de Picardie (east), or rue

Eugène Spuller (west). *Hours:* Tue-Sun 9am-noon. *Métro/ Buses:* same as Square du Temple. *Admission:* free to browse.

Musée de la Chasse et Nature

This unique hunting and nature museum features paintings by Monet, Tiepolo, Rubens, Chardin, and Brueghel, plus tapestries, furniture, and porcelain decorated with hunting/nature scenes. The collection also includes stuffed animals and equipment used by hunters. Housed in the beautiful Mansart-designed Hôtel de Guénégaud (1650), it's worth paying the six francs over our "extremely cheap" guidelines to see the mansion's exquisite interior, even if the museum doesn't interest you. *Address:* 60 rue des Archives (phone 42-77-59-72). *Hours:* Wed-Sun 10am-12:30pm, 1:30pm-5:30pm. *Métro:* Rambuteau (11). *Buses:* 29, 75. *Admission:* 28F.

Musée de l'Histoire de France/Archives Nationale

On a large city block, several interconnecting Hôtel Particulars (built between 1705-09) are now the depositories for the national archives. Highlights from the vast collection include Napoléon's will, the Edict of Nantes, Marie Antoinette's last letter, Louis XVI's diary, and original letters by Joan of Arc, Voltaire, Richelieu, and de Gaulle. The admission fee also gives access to the elaborate apartments of Prince and Princess de Soubise. Across from the entrance on rue des Archives, take a look at the Porte de Clisson tower, the only remains left of a circa-1380 mansion built on this site. *Address:* enter at 60 rue des Francs-Bourgeois or 58 rue des Archives (phone 40-27-60-96). *Hours:* Wed-Mon 1:45pm-5:45pm. *Métro/Buses:* same as Musée de la Chasse et Nature. *Admission:* 15F.

Musée Picasso

This is the largest collection of Picasso's art in one museum. After the famed artist's death in 1973 and a long court battle with his heirs, his art was given to the French government in lieu of death duty payments. Housed in the palatial Hôtel Salé (built in 1656), the museum includes paintings, drawings, sculpture, ceramics, and other creations from every period in his life, plus paintings by Cézanne, Miro, Matisse, Renoir, Degas, and others from Picasso's personal collection. *Address:* 5 rue de Thorigny (phone 42-71-25-21). *Hours:* Wed-Mon 9:30am-5:30pm. *Métro:* Chemin Vert (8), St-Sebastien-Froissart

(8), St-Paul (1). *Buses:* 29, 69, 76, 93, 96. *Admission:* Carte Musées et Monuments.

Musée de l'Histoire de Paris & Hôtel Carnavalet
Housed in the sumptuous Renaissance mansion Hôtel Carnavalet, this collection of furniture, models, paintings, and other objects documents the history of Paris. One wing is devoted to the French Revolution, with models of the guillotine and portraits of famous revolutionaries. The mansion's most famous resident was Madame Sévigné, who recorded 17th-century Paris history through thousands of letters to her children and friends; some letters are on display. Don't miss the mansion's pretty inner courtyards with sculpted hedges, flowers, and statues. *Address:* 23 rue de Sévigné (phone 42-72-21-13). *Hours:* Tue-Sun 10am-5:40pm. *Métro:* St-Paul (1), Chemin Vert (8). *Buses:* 29, 69, 76, 96. *Admission:* Carte Musées et Monuments.

Institut Tessin & Centre Culturel Suedois
Across from the Hôtel Carnavalet in another mansion, the Institut Tessin's small museum details the history of artistic exchanges between France and Sweden. The institute also has a permanent gallery of contemporary Swedish paintings, another galley for exhibitions on Swedish themes, and a library with books about Swedish art. The Swedish cultural center in the same building has free movies, music, theater, lectures, and other events throughout the year. *Address:* 11 rue Payenne (phone 42-71-82-20). *Hours:* Tue-Fri 10am-1pm & 2pm-5pm, Sat-Sun noon-6pm during temporary exhibitions; closed July 14-September 1. *Métro/Buses:* same as Hôtel Carnavalet.

Musée Cognacq-Jay
Housed in the beautiful 15th-century Hôtel Donon is one of the best 18th-century art collections in Paris, bequeathed to the city by Ernest Cognacq and his wife Louise Jay, founders of the Samaritaine department store. It includes works by Boucher, Fragonard, Chardin, Robert, Watteau, and Quentin de la Tour, plus a collection of exquisite furniture, porcelain, jewelry, and other decorative art objects. *Address:* 8 rue Elzévir (phone 40-27-07-21) *Hours:* Tue-Sun 10am-5:40pm. *Métro/Buses:* same as Hôtel Carnavalet. *Admission:* 17.5F, Carte Musées et Monuments.

Centre Culturel Suisse

The Swiss cultural center has a regular schedule of free concerts, lectures, and movies, plus a small art gallery. *Address:* 32-34-38 rue des Francs-Bourgeois (phone 42-71-44-50; 48-87-47-33 for recorded message). *Hours:* Tue-Sun 2pm-7pm. *Métro/Buses:* same as Hôtel Carnavalet.

Église St-Denys-du-St-Sacrément

In the St. Geneviève chapel of this small 1835 church, located a few blocks north of place des Vosges (see 4th arrondissement), you'll find a gorgeous *Pietà* painted by Delacroix in 1844. *Address:* 68 bis rue Turenne. *Métro:* St-Sebastien-Froissart (8). *Buses:* 20, 29, 96.

The front entrance of the Cathèdrale de Notre-Dame, the most famous Gothic cathedral in the world.

4th Arrondissement

The small 4th arrondissement is one of the most interesting and historic sections of Paris. From the Cathédrale de Notre-Dame at its southwest corner to place des Vosges at its northeast corner to the Centre Georges Pompidou on its northwest corner, this arrondissement harbors a wealth of history and sights, including elegant Hôtel Particulars in the Marais district's south half, several museums and art galleries, the massive Hôtel de Ville, Ile St-Louis, and monuments galore.

The boundaries of the 4th arrondissement are rues Rambuteau and des Francs-Bourgeois (north), east side of the Ile de la Cité, Ile St-Louis, Seine River (south), boulevards Bourdon, Beaumarchais, and place de la Bastille (east), and boulevards Sébastopol and du Palais (west).

Cathédrale de Notre-Dame de Paris

Built primarily from 1163 to 1345, with extensive renovations in the 19th century by Viollet-le-Duc (the chief restorationist of medieval monuments and sites throughout France), the incomparable Cathédrale de Notre-Dame is, literally, the center of Paris, since all distances are measured from it. Inside and out, you will marvel at the craftsmanship of the cathedral's construction (used as the principal model for all Gothic cathedrals), the flying buttresses, the unique details in the architectural accents, the sublime 13th-century stained glass rose windows that cast rainbows of light across the stone floor, the small chapels tucked into crannies, beautiful carvings on the three massive entrance portals, the statues above the portals, grotesque gargoyles, and much, much more. Notre-Dame is simply one of the wonders of the world. *Address:* place du Parvis Notre-Dame (phone 43-29-50-40). *Hours:* daily 8am-7pm. *Métro:* Cité (4), St-Michel/Notre-Dame (B, C). *Buses:* 21, 24, 27,

38, 47, 85, 96. *Admission:* free to view sanctuary, chapels, and grounds; free tours in English on Wed, free concerts on Sun and selected times during the year, and free organ recitals daily at 5:45pm. Admission to the Treasury—the collection of 19th-century manuscripts, gold ornaments, and holy relics—is 15F.

Tours des Notre-Dame

Climb the 387 steps to reach the top of the Cathédral's twin towers, where you'll enjoy a magnificent view of Paris, especially over the Ile de la Cité, Seine River, and 5th arrondissement. Take a look at the gargoyles leaning from the building, sneering at all the tourists invading their haunt. This elevated view of the Cathédral's spire, flying buttresses, and plaza is a must. *Address:* steps begin at north tower (phone 43-29-50-40). *Hours:* Oct 1-March 31: daily 9:30am-5pm; April 1-Sep 30: daily 9:30am-6:30pm. *Métro/Buses:* same as Cathédrale de Notre-Dame. *Admission:* Carte Musées et Monuments.

Crypte Archeologique Notre-Dame

Considered the most important archeological crypt in Europe, the excavations (unearthed in 1965 during construction of an underground parking lot) show ruins of 3rd-century Roman buildings and ramparts, 9th-century medieval cellars from Philippe Auguste's castle, and the foundations of a church and children's home. Exhibits with commentary in both French and English detail the evolution of Paris from a Celtic settlement to a Roman city. *Address:* beneath place du Parvis Notre-Dame (phone 43-29-83-51). *Hours:* Oct 1-March 31: daily 10am-5:30pm; April 1-Sep 30: 10am-6pm; closed Jan 1, May 1, Nov 1, Nov 11, Dec 25. *Métro/Buses:* same as Cathédrale de Notre-Dame. *Admission:* Carte Musées et Monuments.

Musée Notre-Dame de Paris

Operated by a Catholic religious association, this small museum traces the history of the Cathédrale de Notre-Dame through art, engravings, medals, documents, and other objects. *Address:* 10 rue du Cloître Notre-Dame (phone 43-25-42-92). *Hours:* Wed, Sat, Sun 2:30pm-6pm; closed Jan 1, Easter Sunday, Pentecost Sunday. *Métro/Buses:* same as Cathédrale de Notre-Dame. *Admission:* 15F.

Square Jean XXIII

With cherry, chestnut, and lime trees, the pretty park behind the Cathédrale de Notre-Dame is a quiet place to relax away from the congested cathedral entrance area, and it offers good views of the flying buttresses. There are occasional free concerts here by a local police precinct's orchestra. *Address:* rue du Cloître Notre-Dame at quai de l'Archevêché. *Métro/Buses:* same as Cathédrale de Notre-Dame.

Mémorial des Martyrs de la Déportation

At the east tip of the Ile de la Cité, across from Square Jean XXIII, a memorial is dedicated to the 200,000 French who died in Nazi concentration camps from 1939 to 1945. From the sidewalk, steps lead down to a dungeon-like cell, where iron bars block the view of the river. Inside the crypt's black chamber are thousands of points of light (quartz crystals imbedded into the wall) representing the dead, ending in a black hole with a single light bulb hanging in the middle, with empty cells on each side. The French motto above the exit reads "Forgive, but don't forget." It's a haunting but important sight, a reminder of the depravity of war and the depths of human wickedness. *Address:* square de l'Ile-de-France (phone 46-33-87-56). *Hours:* April 1-Sep 30: daily 10am-noon & 2pm-7pm; Oct 1-March 31: daily 10am-noon & 2pm-5pm. *Métro:* Cité (4), St-Michel/Notre-Dame (B, C). *Buses:* 24, 47, 67.

Hôtel Dieu

The Hôtel Dieu, one of the oldest and largest public hospitals in Paris, occupies eight square blocks opposite the Cathédrale de Notre-Dame. You can't go on the floors unless you're visiting a patient, but you can explore (quietly) its peaceful inner courtyard. *Address:* 1 place du Parvis Notre-Dame (phone 42-34-82-34). *Hours:* open during daylight hours. *Métro/Buses:* same as Cathédrale de Notre-Dame.

Ile St-Louis

There are no major sights on this small island in the center of Paris unless you consider **Berthillon**, the most popular ice cream parlor in the city (closed Mon and Tue in winter). Rather, the Ile St-Louis is an extension of the Marais district, a quiet and ritzy residential section that has become one of the most sought-after addresses in Paris. Walk down the middle of the island on rue St-Louis-en-l'Ile to find several interesting shops, then circle it on the quais or sidewalks at water level for good views of the Seine River, the Ile de la Cité, and the rear of the Cathédrale de Notre-Dame. *Address:* center of Paris in the Seine River. *Métro:* Pont Marie (7), Sully-Morland (7). *Buses:* 24, 63, 67, 86, 87, 89.

Église St-Louis-en-l'Ile

This is the only church on the Ile St-Louis. It was built from 1664 to 1725 and includes 15th-18th century paintings, sculpture, bas-reliefs, and a modern steeple. *Address:* 19 bis rue St-Louis-en-l'Ile. *Métro/Buses:* same as Ile St-Louis.

Hôtel Lambert

This circa-1640 mansion, home of Voltaire and owned by the Rothschild family since 1972, is used primarily for state functions. It is occasionally open for free public tours. *Address:* 2 rue St-Louis-en-l'Ile. *Métro/Buses:* same as Ile St-Louis.

Hôtel de Lauzan

This beautiful mansion, built by Le Vau in 1656 for a wealthy caterer, is named for its second owner, the Duke of Lauzan, a favorite of King Louis XIV who was sent to the Bastille after his secret marriage was revealed to the King. In the 19th century, Rilke, Wagner, Delacroix, and Baudelaire lived here at various times. In 1928, the city restored it to serve as a residence for visiting dignitaries. When no celebrities are there, the building is open to the public for free on weekends and by special appointment during the week (permission required from the *Chef du Protocole* at the Hôtel de Ville). *Address:* 17 quai d'Anjou. *Hours:* Sat & Sun 10am-5:40pm (when available). *Métro/Buses:* same as Ile St-Louis.

Musée Adam Mickiewicz, Salon Chopin, & Musée Boleslas Biegas

This small museum is devoted to the Polish poet who came to France in 1832 bearing the partitioned non-existence of his homeland. Housed in a few rooms of a 17th-century mansion, its collection features a library with 19th-century Polish newspapers and exhibits on the poet's relationship with his contemporaries. One room is dedicated to Frederic Chopin, including his armchair and the only daguerreotype in the world of the

A barge travels beneath the Pont de la Tournelle connecting the Left Bank to the Ile St-Louis.

composer as a young man. The Musée Boleslas Biegas show-cases late 19th-century and early 20th-century Polish art. There are guided tours on the hour. *Admission:* 30F for all three museums. *Address:* 6 quai d'Orleans on the Ile St-Louis (phone 43-54-35-61). *Hours:* Thur 3pm-6pm; closed July 14-Aug 15. *Métro/Buses:* same as Ile St-Louis.

Pont de la Tournelle
The bridge connecting the Ile St-Louis to the Left Bank at quai de la Tournelle affords excellent views of the rear of the Cathédrale de Notre-Dame. A narrow statue of Ste-Geneviève, atop a rocket-like pedestal, stands on the Left Bank side of the bridge. *Métro:* Pont Marie (7). *Buses:* 24, 67.

Centre Georges Pompidou

The Centre Georges Pompidou—once the city's most contro-versial building with its modern "warehouse" design of ex-posed, brightly painted duct and pipe work (built in 1977)—is now the second most-visited sight in Paris after the Tour Eiffel. It houses the Musée National d'Art Moderne (see below), Bibliothèque Publique d'Information/Video Musiques (a public information library where you can examine books, magazines, audio tapes, slides, and music videos for free), CCI (Centre de Création Industrielle), IRCAM (Institute of Acoustic and Musical Research), Salle Garance (see below), several galleries for tem-porary exhibitions, a computer center, a language lab, a sculp-ture studio, and one of the best art bookstores in Paris. There are excellent views of Paris from its external escalator and rooftop café, plus regular free entertainment from street performers on the outdoor plaza. *Address:* place Georges-Pompidou (phone 42-78-12-33). *Hours:* Mon, Wed-Fri noon-10pm, Sat & Sun 10am-10pm; closed May 1. *Métro:* Rambuteau (11). *Buses:* 29, 38, 47, 75. *Admission:* free to all parts of building except for modern art museum, galleries, Salle Garance, and ongoing exhibitions.

Musée National d'Art Moderne

This museum has one of the largest permanent collections of modern art (1905 to the present) in the world. It includes near-ly every important 20th-century artist and art movement, in-cluding a good representation by the Fauves, Cubists, Sur-realists, Symbolists, Abstractionists, Expressionists, and all the post- and neo-offshoots of these movements. The museum has exhibitions each year honoring famous artists with major retro-spectives of their work. *Address:* floors 3-4, Centre Georges Pompidou. *Hours/Métro/Buses:* same as Centre Georges Pom-pidou. *Admission:* Carte Musées et Monuments.

Salle Garance

At the rear of the Centre Georges Pompidou (main floor), three nondescript theaters offer a variety of movies—and as many as you can stand—all for one price. *Address/Hours/Métro/Buses:* same as Centre Georges Pompidou. *Admission:* 27F (a bargain, considering the average cost of a movie in Paris is 40F).

Fontaine Stravinsky

This fountain on the south end of the Centre Georges Pompidou features garishly colored and bizarre mechanical creatures that gyrate, twirl, and spew water in honor of the works of composer Igor Stravinsky. Our favorite is the big red lips spitting water. Children will love it. *Address:* place Igor Stravinsky. *Métro/ Buses:* same as Centre Georges Pompidou.

Église St-Merri

On the other side of the Fontaine Stravinsky, this 15th-century Flamboyant Gothic church extends into the houses around it. Its interior features a 17th-century organ, elaborately decorated choir and pulpit, a marble crucifix, fine wood bas-reliefs, original stained glass, the oldest bell (1331) in Paris, and two paintings by Van Loo. Free concerts are held here every Saturday (9pm) and Sunday (4pm), except in August. *Address:* enter at 76 rue de la Verrerie (phone 42-76-93-93). *Métro:* Rambuteau (11), Hôtel de Ville (1, 11). *Buses:* 38, 47, 58, 70, 75.

Église St-Paul-St-Louis

The foundation for this church was laid in 1627 by order of King Louis XIII. With Corinthian columns and a balustraded top that resembles a temple, the building's largely Italian design caused great controversy during its construction. The exterior also features a statue of the King framed on the façade of the top level and tall, arched windows. Inside, it's decorated in bright colors and features several outstanding pieces of sculpture and paintings from the 17th to 19th centuries, including works by Vouet and Delacroix. Also inside, look through the small dome to view more outstanding craftsmanship. *Address:* 99 rue St-Antoine. *Métro:* St-Paul (1). *Buses:* 67, 69, 76, 96.

Place du Châtelet

This busy traffic intersection and ancient crossroads (today a main stop for public buses) features a pretty 19th-century fountain celebrating Napoléon's Egyptian campaign, the adjacent Tour St-Jacques (see below), and two famous theaters: **Châtelet** and **Théâtre de la Ville**. *Address:* between quai de la Mégisserie and avenue Victoria. *Métro:* Châtelet (1, 4, 7, 11). *Buses:* 21, 38, 47, 58, 67, 69, 70, 72, 74, 75, 76, 81, 85, 96.

Tour St-Jacques

This 171-foot tower and area landmark is all that's left of the 16th-century Église St-Jacques-la-Boucheries, destroyed by revolutionaries in 1797. The statue at its base is of Pascal, who performed experiments here to determine the weight of air. Today, it's used as a meteorological observatory and is not open to the public. *Address:* on a square between rue de Rivoli and avenue Victoria. *Métro/Buses:* same as place du Châtelet.

Hôtel de Ville (Mairie de Paris)

The Paris city hall, built between 1874-84 on the foundation of a building burned by the 1871 Commune, is set on the end of a large, open square that was used as the municipal execution site. During the French Revolution, a guillotine was employed here. *Address:* place de la Hôtel de Ville (phone 42-76-50-46). *Hours:* Mon-Sat 9am-6pm. *Métro:* Hôtel de Ville (1, 11). *Buses:* 38, 47, 58, 67, 69, 70, 72, 74, 75, 76, 96. *Admission:* free tour on Monday at 10:30am (starts from north porch on rue Lobau), and free exhibits in lobby.

Bazar de l'Hôtel de Ville (BHV)

The BHV is one of the city's most popular department stores, thanks to its large household and hardware departments in the basement. For do-it-yourselfers, it's paradise and a great place to find an inexpensive French gadget as a souvenir. If you need an electrical converter, tools, or straps to fix a broken suitcase, this is the store. *Address:* 52 rue de Rivoli (phone 42-74-90-00). *Hours:* Mon, Tue, Thur-Sat 9:30am-7pm; Wed 9:30am-10pm. *Métro/Buses:* same as Hôtel de Ville.

Église St-Gervais-St-Protais

One of the first churches in Paris was built on this site in the 7th century. The current church, built between 1494 and 1621, reflects the wild Flamboyant Gothic period (flying buttresses and pointed roofs) combined with Classical and Renaissance architectural ideas (an arched roof tower with balustrade and columns). Inside, it has several good statues, paintings (including *Beheading of John the Baptist* by Vignon), and stained glass windows. In 1918, during a Good Friday service, a German shell hit the church, killing 74. *Address:* rue François-Miron at place St-Gervais (behind the Hôtel de Ville). *Métro:* Hôtel de Ville (1, 11). *Buses:* 67, 69, 75, 76, 96.

Memorial du Martyr Juif Inconnu & Centre de Documentation Juive Contemporaire

The bronze monument in the courtyard was built in 1956 for the unknown French Jews who died in Nazi concentration camps. The names of all the camps are listed on it, and the crypt downstairs has an eternal flame burning over ashes brought back from concentration camps and the Warsaw Ghetto. The center has a small Holocaust museum and a library with over 400,000 documents regarding the deportation and the Nazi era in France. *Address:* 17 rue Geoffroy l'Asnier (phone 42-77-44-72). *Hours:* Memorial: Sun-Thur 10am-1pm & 2pm-6pm; Fri 10am-1pm & 2pm-5pm. Center: Mon-Thur 2pm-5:30; closed Jan 1, May 1, Jewish feasts. *Métro:* St-Paul (1), Pont Marie (7). *Buses:* 67, 69, 76, 96. *Admission:* free for memorial and library, 15F for museum.

Hôtel Sens & Bibliothèque Forney

The Archbishop of Sens' residence, with its fortress-style architecture, is considered one of the best-preserved medieval mansions in Paris. Built from 1474-1507, it has a dungeon in the square courtyard tower, overhanging corner turrets protruding from the building (a defense measure for looking out over the streets for invaders), and a pretty hedge and flower garden. The Forney library has a permanent collection of paintings, wall paper, posters, and decorative arts books. *Address:* 1 rue du Figuier (phone 42-78-14-60). *Hours:* Tue-Sat 1:30pm-8pm. *Métro:* Pont Marie (7). *Bus:* 67. *Admission:* 15F.

Village St-Paul

The Village St-Paul, occupying an entire block between the Seine River and rue Charlemagne, is an intriguing antique and art gallery district, perfect for an afternoon of browsing. *Address:* rue St-Paul. *Hours:* Thur-Mon 9am-6pm. *Métro:* Pont Marie (7), Sully-Morland (7). *Buses:* 67, 69, 96.

Ancient City Wall

The largest surviving section of the fortified city wall (with two towers), built by order of King Philippe Auguste (1180-1223), is found here incorporated into the wall of the Lycée Charlemagne (secondary school). You can see another section in the 5th arrondissement near the Panthéon. *Address:* rue des Jardins-St-Paul. *Métro:* Sully-Morland (7). *Buses:* 67.

Galerie Agathe Gaillard

The first photography gallery in Paris, it remains one of the best. Masters like Adams, Cartier-Bresson, Doisneau, and Riboud have exhibited here, along with top contemporary French photographers. *Address:* 3 rue du Pont-Louis-Philippe (phone 42-77-38-24). *Hours:* Tue-Sat 1pm-7pm. *Métro:* Pont Marie (7). *Buses:* 67, 69, 76, 96.

Place des Vosges

This is the oldest and most perfect square in Paris. Constructed by Henri IV from 1605 to 1612, it was a model for urban construction throughout Europe. Today, the park that occupies its interior has a statue of King Louis XIII at its center, fountains at each corner, and a regular group of mothers and children. The 36 slender brick townhouses that enclose the square on three sides have been restored as residences. Shops and restaurants operate under the arched, street-level arcades. *Address:* crossed by rue des Francs-Bourgeois (north) and access via rue de Birangue off rue St-Antoine (south). *Métro:* Bastille (1, 5, 8), Chemin Vert (8). *Buses:* 20, 29, 65, 69, 76, 86, 87, 91, 96.

Maison de Victor Hugo

This museum, housed in the prolific author's apartment where he lived from 1832 to 1848 (and which he personally decorated), features an interesting collection of Hugo memorabilia, including drawings, photographs, furniture, first-edition books, and exhibits on his life. The museum also hosts exhibitions on the literature of Hugo's time. *Address:* 6 place des Vosges (phone 42-72-10-16). *Hours:* Tue-Sun 10am-5:40pm. *Métro/Buses:* same as Place des Vosges. *Admission:* 17.5F, Carte Musées et Monuments.

Bibliothèque Historique de la Ville de Paris

The main Paris public library is housed in the Hôtel de Lamoignon, an elegant mansion built in 1584 for Diane de France, daughter of King Henri II. Among its books are several interesting picture texts of Paris during past centuries. *Address:* 24 rue Pavée (phone 42-27-10-18). *Hours:* Mon-Sat 9:30am-6pm. *Métro:* St-Paul (1), Chemin Vert (8). *Buses:* 29, 69, 76, 96. *Admission:* free to enter and use materials in reading room. Present your passport and request a reader's card.

Crédit Municipal

If you've blown your travel budget, this city-operated pawn shop will provide loans on items valued over 500F. They also hold public auctions of unclaimed items two or three times per month, offering a good selection of jewelry, silverware, bric-a-brac, cameras, and paintings. Though the buyer must pay a tax of 17.29% on any items bought, you can find extremely cheap goods here. *Address:* 53 bis rue des Francs-Bourgeois (phone 42-71-25-43). *Hours:* Mon-Fri 9am-6pm. *Métro/Buses:* same as Musée Kwok-On.

Place de la Bastille

This congested traffic intersection, where the 4th, 11th, and 12th arrondissements converge, is identified by the *Colonne de Juillet* (July Column), a 170-foot high monument with a winged Mercury at its top, which commemorates both the demolition of the Bastille in July 1789 by a mob and the July Uprising of 1830. The outline of the prison is marked on paving stones on the southwest corner, and the names of the revolutionaries killed here are etched on the shaft of the monument. During the annual Bastille Day (July 14) celebration, there's a wild party at this sight. And from the southeast corner, take a look at the gleaming, curved façade of the new opera building (see 12th arrondissement). *Address:* entered by 12 streets including rues St-Antoine, du Faubourg-St-Antoine, and de Lyon, and boulevards Henri IV, Richard Lenoir, and Beaumarchais. *Métro:* Bastille (1, 5, 8). *Buses:* 20, 29, 65, 69, 76, 86, 87, 91.

Hôtel Béthune-Sully

Within this 17th-century mansion is the main office for the *Caisse Nationale des Monuments Historiques et des Sites*, the organization responsible for administering historic monuments and sites in France. The mansion's dual courtyards (with passage through the buildings) provides a shortcut from rue St-Antoine to the southwest corner of place des Vosges. *Address:* 62 rue St-Antoine (phone 44-61-21-69). *Hours:* Courtyards: daily 9am-7pm. Guided tours of mansion: Sat & Sun at 3pm; closed Jan 1, May 1, Nov 1, Nov 11, Dec 25. *Métro:* St-Paul (1), Bastille (1, 5, 8). *Buses:* 69, 76, 96. *Admission:* Courtyards, information center, and bookshops: free.

Garde Républicaine

This small museum in the headquarters of the Republican Guard has military souvenirs depicting its history from 1802 to the present. The cavalry honor guard, with its fancy uniforms and plumed hats, is still on call for state functions and parades. If you're here on a holiday, you might get to see them in action. Otherwise, peek through the courtyard door in the early morning, when trainers exercise the horses. *Address:* 18 boulevard Henri IV (phone 42-76-13-23). *Hours:* Mon-Fri 8am-noon & 2pm-6pm by appointment only (six months in advance!); closed August. *Métro:* Bastille (1, 5, 8), Sully-Morland (7). *Buses:* 67, 86, 87.

Pavillon de l'Arsenal

Inside the former arsenal building, a series of exhibits, photographs, plans, and models describe Paris's current architectural projects and how past developments have evolved. One of the highlights is a huge, illuminated model of Paris showing all its landmarks. *Address:* 21 boulevard Morland (phone 42-76-33-97). *Hours:* Tue-Sat 10:30am-6:30pm, Sun 11am-7pm. *Métro:* Sully-Morland (7). *Buses:* 67, 86, 87.

Bibliothèque Arsenal

Once the weapon and powder factory of Henri IV, this building has been a public library since 1797. Literary greats like Lamartine, Dumas, and Hugo were often seen reading books here. Its current collection includes two million books, 15,000 manuscripts, 120,000 prints, and 17th-century paintings in ornately decorated rooms. *Address:* 1-3 rue de Sully (phone 42-77-44-21). *Hours:* Mon-Sat 10:30am-5:30pm. *Métro/Buses:* same as Pavillon de l'Arsenal. *Admission:* 3F for reading card.

5th Arrondissement

The 5th arrondissement is a mecca for students, scholars, artists, writers, musicians, and other creative types. The eastern half of the famed Left Bank and soul of the Latin Quarter, its highlights include the Sorbonne, Panthéon, a few outstanding churches, Roman remains, Jardins des Plantes, several small museums, rue Mouffetard street market, music clubs, and some of the best low-cost restaurants and hotels in the city.

The 5th is also one of the largest arrondissements in central Paris. Its boundaries are Seine River (north), boulevards de Port Royal and St-Marcel (south), boulevard l'Hôpital (east), and boulevard St-Michel (west).

Boulevard St-Michel

The wide and long boulevard St-Michel (or "Boul Mich," as it's called by students), created by Haussmann in the mid-1800's, divides the 5th and 6th arrondissements. Running from the Seine River and Ile de la Cité, it travels south up a long hill to cross boulevard St-Germain, then continues past the Jardin du Luxembourg to boulevard Montparnasse. All along this route, you'll discover numerous shops, cafés, and restaurants—many catering to the tastes and budgets of students attending the universities in the area. *Métro:* St-Michel (4, C), St-Michel/Notre-Dame (B, C), Cluny-La Sorbonne (10), Luxembourg (B), Port Royal (B). *Buses:* 21, 27, 38, 81, 84, 85.

Rue de la Huchette

The narrow, pedestrians-only rue de la Huchette has changed a lot since it was the stomping grounds of the "Lost Generation" writers of the 1920's and "Beat" writers of the 1950's. Today, it's filled with students seeking inexpensive meals at Greek and Turkish restaurants lining the street. *Address:* between boule-

vard St-Michel and rue du Petit-Pont. *Métro/Buses:* same as
Boulevard St-Michel.

Rue du Chat-qui-Pêche
The "street of the cat who fishes" is just eight feet wide and
hardly half a block long. Parisians claim this medieval alley is
the narrowest short street (or shortest narrow street?) in the
world. *Address:* between quai St-Michel and rue de la Huchette. *Métro/Buses:* same as Boulevard St-Michel.

Shakespeare & Company
The current version of the famous bookstore—owned by Sylvia
Beach and a meeting place for Hemingway, Fitzgerald, Pound,
Stein, dos Passos, Joyce, and other literary greats—is in a different location from the original store that gained such renown,
but it's still a haven for writers and their groupies. It offers regular free poetry readings and sells English-language books, each
stamped with the company logo. *Address:* 37 rue de la Bû-
cherie. *Hours:* daily noon-midnight. *Métro:* St-Michel/Notre-
Dame (B, C). *Buses:* 24, 47.

Square René-Viviani & Église St-Julien-le-Pauvre
The city's oldest tree, a *robinier false acacia* planted in 1601,
grows on the pretty square René-Viviani, which offers good
views of the Cathédrale de Notre-Dame. On the southwest corner of the square, the Église St-Julien-le-Pauvre, a small Gothic
church built from 1170-1240 (with 17th-century alterations) features an outstanding organ and some interesting stained glass
windows. *Address:* 1 rue St-Julien-le-Pauvre. *Métro:* St-Michel/
Notre-Dame (B, C). *Buses:* 24.

Église St-Séverin
Not far from the Église St-Julien-le-Pauvre is one of the loveliest
small Gothic churches in Paris. Begun in the 13th century and
rebuilt in 1450 after a fire (with extensions in the 16th and 17th
centuries), the Église St-Séverin features original stained glass
windows, medieval paintings, a lavishly decorated 18th-centu-
ry organ (one of the world's largest, with 6,588 pipes), and exquisite ornamentation associated with the Gothic period. *Address:* 1 rue des Prêtres-St-Séverin. *Métro:* St-Michel/Notre-
Dame (B, C). *Buses:* 21, 24, 27, 38, 67, 81, 85, 96.

Abbey Bookshop

Along with selling used English-language books for extreme-ly cheap prices, this Canadian-owned bookstore offers free coffee to its customers—a great bargain, as you know if you've ever ordered coffee at a Paris restaurant. *Address:* 29 rue de la Parcheminerie (phone 46-33-16-24). *Hours:* Mon-Thur 11am-10pm, Fri-Sat 11am-midnight, Sun noon-10pm. *Métro:* St-Michel/Notre-Dame (B,C), Cluny-La Sorbonne (10). *Buses:* 24, 34, 47, 85, 87.

Aux Vieux Campeur

For a unique sight, peek into the window of the largest outfitter of camping and mountain-climbing in France (it occupies an entire block), where you'll see prospective mountaineers climbing an indoor version of the Eiger's North Face. If outdoor pursuits are near to your heart, you'll love this store, an adven-ture in itself. *Address:* 48 rue des Écoles (phone 43-29-12-32). *Hours:* Mon 2pm-7pm, Tue-Sat 9:30am-8pm. *Métro:* Cluny-La Sorbonne (10), Maubert-Mutualité (10). *Buses:* 63, 86, 87.

Musée des Collections Historiques de la Prefecture de Police

Inside the 5th arrondissement's police headquarters, a small museum details the history of Paris's police force from 1563 to the present. Its collection includes uniforms, weapons, prison registers, royal warrants, and papers documenting famous cases. *Address:* enter at 1 bis rue des Carmes or 4 rue de la Mon-taigne-Ste-Geneviève; upstairs from the lobby (phone 44-41-52-50). *Hours:* Mon-Fri 9am-5pm, Sat 10am-5pm. *Métro:* Maubert-Mutualité (10). *Buses:* 24, 47, 63, 86, 87.

Église St-Nicolas-du-Chardonnet

The richly decorated choir chapel and several paintings in this small 17th-century church are attributed to the painter and dec-orator Charles Le Brun, whose tomb is here. Above the tomb, there's a life-size bust of the artist in front of an obelisk shaped like a pyramid. In another chapel is the tomb of Bignon, who started the Bibliothèque Nationale. The church also has a paint-ing by Corot in the first chapel on the right and a Brueghel painting in the sacristy. *Address:* 30 rue St-Victor. *Métro:* Mau-bert-Mutualité (10). *Buses:* 24, 47, 63, 86, 87.

Palais de la Mutualité

Free concerts are held during the summer at this art deco building. *Address:* next to Église St-Nicolas-du-Chardonnet. *Métro/ Buses:* same as Église St-Nicolas-du-Chardonnet.

Grand Action Rive/Action Écoles

These theaters shows one classic film Mon-Sat at 12:10pm, and the price (30F) is a bargain. *Address:* 5 rue des Écoles/23 rue des Écoles. *Métro:* Cardinal Lemoine (10). *Buses:* 47, 63, 67, 87, 89.

Musée du Moyen Age (formerly Musée de Cluny) & Thermes de Cluny

In the lower level of the 15th-century Hôtel de Cluny are the remains of 3rd-century Gallo-Roman thermal baths—the best examples of ancient Paris. The galleries in the rest of the building contain the most important collection of medieval art and historic objects in France, including weapons, paintings, sculpture, furniture, tapestries, and jewelry. There are also fragments from 21 heads of the Kings Gallery, torn from Cathédrale de Notre-Dame (and stolen) during the French Revolution, only to be rediscovered in 1977 during the renovation of a 9th arrondissement hotel. *Address:* 6 place Paul-Painlevé (phone 43-25-62-00). *Hours:* Wed-Mon 9:15am-5:45pm. *Métro:* Cluny/La Sorbonne (10). *Buses:* 21, 27, 38, 63, 85, 86, 87. *Admission:* 18F on Sunday, Carte Musées et Monuments.

Sorbonne

Founded in 1253 by Robert de Sorbon as a small theology school for 16 students, the Sorbonne quickly became the most powerful institution of higher learning in France, a reputation it holds today. In the school's chapel (built 1635-42), you'll find the tomb of one of its graduates, the ruthless Cardinal Richelieu, with his red hat suspended above him from the ceiling. The Sorbonne occupies several blocks and consists of Paris Universités I, III, and IV. *Address:* main entrance at place de la Sorbonne; other entrances off rue des Écoles (north), rue Cujas (south), rue St-Jacques (east), and rue Victor Cousin (west). *Métro:* Cluny/La Sorbonne (10). *Buses:* 21, 27, 38, 63, 81, 85, 86, 87. *Admission:* free to wander down its halls (but try to blend in with the students). No admittance to classes. The church and chapel are open only during cultural events, temporary exhibitions, and special church services.

Collège de France

Not as exclusive as the Sorbonne, this college was founded in 1530 by King Francis I as *Collège du Roi* (College of the King) as an alternative to the more theologically biased Sorbonne, which tended to execute intellectual authority over the royalty. Today, the college has numerous buildings spread throughout the 5th arrondissement. *Address:* 11 place Berthelot. *Métro:* Cluny/La Sorbonne (10), Maubert/Mutualité (10). *Buses:* 63, 86, 87. *Admission:* Free to sit in on classes and lectures. Students with an international student ID card can eat in the school's cafeterias (extremely cheap).

Rue St-Jacques

This is the oldest paved street in Paris. During medieval times, it was the beginning of one of the main pilgrimage roads to the shrine of St. Jacques at Santiago de Campostela in northwest Spain, a 1,000-mile trek from Paris. With few buses on it, it's still a fine road for walking. *Address:* between Église St-Séverin and boulevard de Port Royal. *Métro:* St-Michel/Notre-Dame (B, C), Luxembourg (B), Port Royal (B). *Buses:* 24, 47.

Centre de la Mer et Des Eaux

Films about the work of Jacques Cousteau are shown at this oceanographic museum. *Address:* 195 rue Saint-Jacques (phone 46-33-08-61). *Hours:* Tue-Fri 10am-12:30pm, 1:15pm-5:30pm, Sat-Sun 10am-5:30pm; closed Monday and holidays. *Métro:* Luxembourg (B). *Buses:* 21, 27. *Admission:* 15F for films; museum is 25F.

Panthéon

The Panthéon, a church built for Louis XV atop the highest hill on the Left Bank, was patterned after the Pantheon in Rome. Its dome is a Paris landmark. Inside, it's a mausoleum of the great men of France, with the tombs of writers/philosophers Voltaire, Hugo, Zola, Rousseau, and Mirabeau, scientists Braille and Berthelot, Jean Jaurès (founder of France's socialist party), explorer Bouganville, Jean Moulin (a World War II Resistance leader), and architect Soufflot. *Address:* place du Panthéon (phone 43-54-34-51). *Hours:* Oct 1-March 31: daily 10am-5:30pm; April 1-Sep 30 9:30am-6:30pm; closed Jan 1, May 1, Nov 1, Nov 11, Dec 25. *Métro:* Luxembourg (B). *Buses:* 21, 27,

The Gothic-Renaissance Église St-Étienne-du-Mont

38, 63, 82, 84, 85, 87, 89. *Admission:* Carte Musées et Monuments.

Église St-Étienne-du-Mont

Almost lost in the shadow of the Panthéon, the Église St-Étienne-du-Mont is a highly original church with a unique mixture of Gothic and Renaissance architectural elements. Built in phases from 1492 to 1626, it features a tall, domed clock tower, spiral stone staircases with lattice-style railings winding around columns, the only rood screen (an ornamented altar screen shielding choir from nave) in Paris, a circa-1650 carved wood pulpit supported by a figure of Samson, a Baroque organ, numerous 17th-century paintings, and some of the best stained glass windows in town. *Address:* place Ste-Geneviève. *Métro:* Cardinal Lemoine (10). *Buses:* 84, 89.

Rue Mouffetard

For a good look at a medieval Paris street, follow the narrow, cobblestone rue Mouffetard down a long hill from place de la Contrescarpe to the Église St-Médard (see below). This path features one of the city's oldest and most colorful street markets, numerous small shops and service businesses, restaurants, cafés, and a bowling alley (see below). *Address:* access from several streets off rue Monge. *Métro:* Cardinal Lemoine (10), Monge (7), Censier Daubenton (7). *Buses:* 27, 47.

Bowling Mouffetard

This is the cheapest place to bowl and play billiards in Paris, favored by students living in the area. It also has a bar and restaurant. *Address:* 73 rue Mouffetard. *Hours:* daily 10am-2am. *Métro:* Monge (7). *Buses:* 47. *Admission:* 20F for bowling (another 18F for shoes), less for billiards and video games.

Église St-Médard

At the bottom of the rue Mouffetard hill, there's a small 15th-century church featuring a Renaissance decorated choir, circa-1644 Baroque organ, 17th- and 18th-century paintings, and a nice park. The church was famous as a pilgrimage destination, since the Jansenist François Paris (who had a reputation for healing powers; died 1727) laid in its cemetery. Once the word got out, countless sick and disabled people came here to worship at his grave, hoping for a miraculous cure. Due to the mob scene and con artists claiming the same powers, the military closed the cemetery in 1732, removing it permanently in the early 19th century. *Address:* 141 rue Mouffetard. *Métro:* Censier Daubenton (7). *Buses:* 27, 47.

Arènes de Lutèce

This 325-foot by 425-foot oval amphitheater, along with the Cluny baths and the excavations beneath place du Parvis Notre-Dame, are the only visible remains of the Gallo-Roman period in Paris. Once used for theatrical performances, the arena could seat 17,000 people—slightly smaller than Rome's Colosseum. Abandoned in the 3rd century, it was used as a quarry until rediscovered in 1869. Today it's a park, a good place to picnic and watch the *boules* matches. *Address:* 47 rue Monge, with other entrances off rues de Navarre and des Arènes. *Hours:* summer: daily 8am-10pm; winter: 8am-5:30pm. *Métro:* Cardinal Lemoine (10), place Monge (7), Jussieu (7, 10). *Buses:* 47, 67.

La Mosquée et Institut Musulman

Complete with minaret, the city's Moslem temple has sunken gardens, tiled patios, courtyards, Turkish baths (available to the public, but expensive), a library, a *salon de thé,* and a restaurant. *Address:* place du Puits de L'Ermite. *Hours:* guided tours: Mon-Thur, Sat, Sun 9am-noon & 2pm-6pm; closed on Moslem holidays. *Métro:* Monge (7), Censier Daubenton (7). *Buses:* 24, 47, 57, 61, 63, 67, 89. *Admission:* 15F.

Jardin des Plantes

Founded in 1640 to grow medicinal herbs to promote King Louis XIII's health, the pleasant Jardin des Plantes is the second-largest park on the Left Bank. (Only the Champ de Mars fronting the Tour Eiffel is larger.) It contains several tree- and flower-lined paths for peaceful strolling, a botanical school with over 10,000 labeled plants, a winter garden with tropical plants, an alpine garden (plants from mountain and polar regions), a library, the oldest public zoo in France, and the Galerie de l'Evolution. The park's Musée Histoire Naturelle has four departments: entomology, paleontology, paleobotany, and mineralogy. *Address:* enter off quai St-Bernard or place Valhubert (north), rue Geoffroy St-Hilaire (south), rue Buffon (east), or rue Cuvier (west) (phone

49-79-30-00). *Hours:* Mon & Wed-Fri 10am-5pm; Sat, Sun 11am-6pm. *Métro:* Gare d'Austerlitz (5, 10, C), Jussieu (7, 10). *Buses:* 24, 57, 61, 63, 65, 67, 89, 91. *Admission:* free for park and library; 15-40F for zoo, museums, and special gardens.

Musée de la Sculpture en Plein Air

Located across the street from the Jardin des Plantes, this open-air museum and park along the Seine River features modern and contemporary sculpture by the likes of Brancusi, César, Schöffer, Stahly, Zadkine, and several contemporary sculptors. On a sunny day, it's an excellent place to picnic, relax, enjoy the art, and watch the river traffic. *Address:* square Tino Rossi; steps lead down to it from quai St-Bernard (phone 43-26-91-90). *Hours:* open 24 hours. *Métro:* Gare d'Austerlitz (5, 10, C). *Buses:* 24, 63, 86, 87, 89.

Les Comptoirs de la Tour d'Argent

If you don't splurge for a meal at La Tour d'Argent, cross the street to its boutique, where you can buy a souvenir with the restaurant's emblem on it. Prices start at few francs for mustard or tea to several thousand francs for an 18th-century bottle of wine. *Address:* 2 rue du Cardinal Lemoine at quai de la Tour-nelle (phone 43-54-23-31). *Hours:* Tue-Sun noon-12:30am. *Métro/Buses:* same as La Petit Musée de la Table.

Musée de l'Assistance Publique

Mostly overlooked by tourists, this interesting museum documents the history of Paris's hospitals from 1630 to the present. Housed in the large 17th-century Hôtel Miramion, its collection includes Roman medicine vials, pewter syringes, uniforms, physicians' instruments, re-created surgery/hospital rooms, and a unique night deposit box created by a convent for abandoned babies. *Address:* 47 quai de la Tournelle (phone 40-27-50-05). *Hours:* Wed-Sun 10am-5pm; closed August. *Métro:* Maubert-Mutualité (10), St-Michel/Notre-Dame (B, C). *Buses:* 24, 47, 63, 86, 87, 88. *Admission:* 20F.

Musée Institut du Monde Arabe

Overlooking the Seine River, this modern glass and aluminum building belongs to the Institut du Monde Arabe, an organization that promotes cultural exchange between France and 18

Arabic nations. Its museum has a post-1950's art collection and other exhibits focusing on Arab-Islamic civilization from the 7th to the 19th centuries. Even if you're not interested in this culture, go to the building to see the south exterior wall, which has 242 electro-photographic diaphragms that adjust to the sun to create evenly filtered light inside. And from the café terrace on the rooftop (take the elevator to the 9th floor), there are panoramic views of the Seine River, the islands, and other parts of Paris. *Address:* 1 rue des Fosses St-Bernard at quai St-Bernard (phone 40-51-38-38). *Hours:* Tue-Sun 10am-6pm; closed Jan 1, May 1, Dec 25. *Métro:* Cardinal-Lemoine (10), Jussieu (7, 10), Sully-Morland (7). *Buses:* 24, 63, 67, 86, 87, 89. *Admission:* free for library and terrace. Carte Musées et Monuments for museum.

6th Arrondissement

The 6th arrondissement is the more colorful half of the famed Left Bank, due partly to its celebrity cafés, national art school, and chic boutiques in the St-Germain-de-Prés quarter. It's also one of the best areas to see medieval Paris, since the narrow maze of streets from the Seine River quais to the boulevard St-Germain have remained relatively unchanged for centuries. In addition, the 6th is home to the large Jardin du Luxemborg, several small museums, and some of the best restaurants in the city.

The boundaries of the 6th arrondissement are Seine River (north), boulevard Montparnasse (south), rues de Sèvres and des Sts-Pères (west), and boulevard St-Michel (east).

Fontaine St-Michel
This enormous fountain, with several levels of cascading water and a sculpture of St. Michel fighting a dragon, is a popular spot for students and modern bohemians. *Address:* place St-Michel. *Métro:* St-Michel (4, C). *Buses:* 24, 27, 84, 85, 96.

Pont des Arts
This narrow, pedestrians-only footbridge is the oldest iron bridge in France and a favorite locale for artists, who enjoy painting the views of the Ile de la Cité. Built in 1803 as a toll bridge, it connects the Institut de France to the south side of the Musée du Louvre. *Address:* place de Institut and quai du Louvre. *Métro:* Pont Neuf (7). *Buses:* 24, 67, 69, 72, 73, 74, 81.

Institut de France & Academie Française
Since 1795, the domed Institut de France building has been the home for the foremost official academic and artistic group in France. Its five academies cover language and literature (founded by Richelieu in 1635), literary history and inscriptions (founded 1663), natural sciences (1666), fine arts (1795), and

moral and political sciences (1832). Election to the elite academy—membership is limited to 40 people—is one of the country's highest honors. On the tour, you'll see the Academie's council chamber, Mazarin Chapel (built 1805), ceremonial hall, and photographs of past winners. *Address:* 21-25 quai de Conti (phone 44-41-44-41). *Hours:* Sat & Sun 10am-3pm by appointment only. *Métro:* Pont-Neuf (7). *Buses:* 24, 27.

Musée Monnaie de Paris

The national mint, set in an imposing 18th-century mansion, has a large display of coins, stamps, tools, molds, documents, engravings, and paintings. Although currency is now made in Pessac (near Bordeaux), this mint still makes weights, medals, and beautiful limited-edition coins. *Address:* 11 quai de Conti (phone 40-46-55-33). *Hours:* Tue & Thur-Sun 1pm-6pm; Wed 1pm-9pm. On Tue & Fri from 2:15pm-2:45pm, you may watch the craftsmen at work. *Métro:* Pont-Neuf (7), St-Michel (4, C). *Buses:* 24, 27, 58, 70. *Admission:* 20F, Carte Musées et Monuments.

Boulevard St-Germain

The multi-lane boulevard St-Germain is one of the longest and busiest streets in Paris. As the main thoroughfare through the heart of the 5th and 6th arrondissements (and a corner of the 7th), it's a shopper's and restaurant-hopper's delight. *Address:* from quai Anatole-France by the Palais Bourbon to quai de Tournelle by the Institut du Monde Arabe. *Métro:* 7th: Assemblée Nationale (12), Solférino (12), Rue du Bac (12); 6th: St-Germain-des-Prés (4), Mabillon (10), Odéon (4, 10); 5th: La Cluny/Sorbonne (10), Maubert-Mutualité (10). *Buses:* 24, 63, 67, 69, 83, 84, 86, 87, 95.

St-Germain-des-Prés Quartier

This quarter, the heart of the Left Bank, features charming, narrow, medieval streets filled with galleries, quaint restaurants, and chic shops frequented by the Paris literary and artistic set. The rues Jacob, de Seine, and Bonaparte are some of the more interesting side streets to explore. *Address:* approximate boundaries are Seine River (north), boulevard St-Germain at the Église St-Germain-des-Prés and Les Deux Magots café (south), rue

Seine (east), and rue des Sts-Pères (west). *Métro:* St-Germain-des-Prés (4), Mabillon (10), Odéon (4, 10). *Buses:* 24, 27, 39, 48, 58, 63, 70, 86, 87, 95, 96.

Église St-Germain-des-Prés

This is the oldest church in Paris. Its current foundation dates to 990, its bell tower to 1014. Inside the Romanesque structure are some interesting 19th-century frescoes by Flandrin, a student of Ingres. In the adjoining church yard, you can view a Picasso statue of poet Guillaume Apollinaire (1880-1918), whose writing influenced the Symbolist and Surrealist movements. *Address:* 3 place St-Germain-des-Prés. *Hours:* daily 10am-5pm. *Métro:* St-Germain-des-Prés (4). *Buses:* 39, 48, 63, 86, 87, 95, 96.

Musée Eugéne Delacroix

In the last home and studio occupied by Delacroix (1858-63), a small museum exhibits minor works and mementos of the great artist. (Better paintings are in the Louvre and many Paris churches.) In the middle of the street opposite the museum, check out the smallest square in Paris. *Address:* 6 rue de Furstenberg (phone 43-54-04-87). *Hours:* Wed-Mon 9:45am-5pm; closed Jan 1, May 1, July 14, Aug 15, Dec 25. *Métro:* St-Germain-des Prés (4), Mabillon (10). *Buses:* 39, 48, 63, 95. *Admission:* 15F, Carte Musées et Monuments.

École Nationale Supérieure des Beaux-Arts

The School of Fine Arts, housed in the circa-1608 Petits Augustins Convent, continues the traditions begun by the 17th-century Royal Academy. You may peek inside its classrooms and studios in search of future master artists and visit the school's gallery. *Address:* 14 rue Bonaparte (phone 47-03-50-00). *Hours:* Mon-Fri 8am-8pm; closed August. *Métro:* St-Germain-des-Prés (4). *Buses:* 24, 27, 39, 48, 68, 95. *Admission:* 20F.

Rue de Buci & Rue Seine

The best street food market in the 6th arrondissement is along the narrow rue Buci. Nearby, rue Seine is known for its excellent art galleries, restaurants, and interesting shops. *Hours:* Tue-Sun 8am-7:30pm. *Métro:* Mabillon (10). *Buses:* 58, 67, 68, 70, 86, 96.

Carrefour de Buci

This wide space between several narrow streets was the site of a gallows in the 18th century and of a guillotine during the French Revolution. Today, the only things cut here are flowers at the daily flower market, an extension of rue Buci food market. *Address:* rue de Buci at rue Mazarine. *Métro/Buses:* same as rue Buci.

Procope

Procope is the oldest restaurant (circa 1686) in Paris still operating in the same location. Franklin, Jefferson, Napoléon, Robespierre, Balzac, Hugo, Sartre, Beauvoir, and Mitterand—it's had its share of famous diners. Unfortunately, its prices are beyond "extremely cheap." Nonetheless, it's a Paris landmark that you should note if you're exploring the maze of medieval streets in the area. You might even spot a celebrity! *Address:* 13 rue de l'Ancienne-Comédie. *Métro:* Odéon (4, 10). *Buses:* 58, 63, 70, 86, 87, 89, 96.

Cour de Rohan

Off this narrow passage, you can peer into three cloistered courtyards that were a part of the 15th-century Archbishops of Rouen's Hôtel Particulier. The walk through the passages and streets to get here takes you into a medieval past, when most Paris streets had similar appearances. *Address:* access off rue de l'Ancienne-Comédie via cour du Commerce-St-André, or off rue de l'Eperon via rue Jardinet. *Métro/Buses:* same as Procope.

Musée-Librairie du Compagnonnage

Housed in the former headquarters of the carpenters' guild *Devoir de Liberté*, this tiny museum documents the history of carpentry guilds in Paris. The popular bistro **Aux Charpentiers** is next door. *Address:* 10 rue Mabillon (phone 43-26-25-03). *Hours:* Mon-Fri 2pm-6pm. *Métro:* Mabillon (10). *Buses:* 63, 70, 86, 87, 96.

Marché St-Germain

The site of the former St-Germain covered market has become a modern mall with American and French chain stores. The market's basement-level swimming pool is still there, though. *Address:* rue Mabillon at rue Clément. *Hours:* daily 9am-9pm. *Métro/Buses:* same as Musée-Librairie du Compagnonnage.

Institut Français de l'Architecuture

This professional association holds temporary exhibitions featuring individual architects or architectural trends, with displays of plans, models, and photographs. If you're curious about a particular building, the association is a good source of information about the architecture of Paris. *Address:* 6 rue de Tournon. *Hours:* Tue-Sat 10:30am-7pm. *Métro/Buses:* same as Musée-Librairie du Compagnonnage.

Couvent des Cordeliers & Musée Dupuytren

This building was the 13th-15th century refectory of the former Cordeliers convent and home of the revolutionary *Club des Cordeliers* (Danton and Robespierre were members). Today, it's used for temporary exhibitions on art and history, and there's a small museum dedicated to pathology and surgery housed within the convent. Its collection of medical instruments dates to 1820. *Address:* 15 rue de l'Ecole de Médecine (phone 40-46-05-47). *Hours:* Tue-Sun 10am-7pm for exhibitions; museum hours Mon-Fri 9:30am-11am & 2pm-4:30pm. *Métro:* Odéon (4, 10), Cluny/La Sorbonne (10). *Buses:* 21, 27, 38, 63, 86, 87, 96. *Admission:* free to 25F (varies depending on exhibition) for convent; 20F for Musée Dupuytren.

Musée de la Histoire de la Médecine

In the Université Paris medical school, a small museum displays a collection of old surgical instruments and hosts temporary exhibitions about medical subjects. *Address:* 12 rue de l'Ecole-de-Medecine (phone 40-46-16-93). *Hours:* Mon-Fri 2pm-5:30pm, Sat 2pm-5pm; closed Dec 25-Jan 1. *Métro/Buses:* same as Couvent des Cordeliers. *Admission:* 20F.

Église St-Sulpice

The Église St-Sulpice, built from 1646-1756, is the largest church on the Left Bank. With a Classical entrance accented by large Corinthian and Doric columns, its Italian-inspired, unadorned exterior seems odd in Gothic-dominated Paris. Although the exterior is plain, the interior is sumptuous: an elaborately decorated pulpit, an 18th-century organ with interesting bas-relief carvings, frescoes by Delacroix, paintings by Van Loo, a richly decorated altar in the Lady Chapel, and a unique sundial in the shape of an obelisk. When the sundial is struck by light, it casts a shadow on a meridian line etched into the floor, making it possible to determine the exact moment of the winter and summer solstices.

On the spacious square opposite the church, a large Visconti fountain consists of four French preachers (Bossuet, Fénelon, Massillon, and Fléchier) sitting inside a temple atop cascading pools of water surrounded by lions. *Address:* place St-Sulpice. *Métro:* St-Sulpice (4). *Buses:* 63, 70, 84, 86, 87, 96.

Jardin du Luxembourg & Palais du Luxembourg

This is the prettiest park on the Left Bank. Within its 60 acres are numerous flower gardens, fountains (including the grotto-like *Fontaine de Medicis* on the northeast corner), statues, large pools where children sail boats, rows of trees for peaceful strolling, and free concerts on Sunday in the band shell. Unlike American parks, you may not sit or play on the grass here, and specific areas are reserved for individual activities. At the park's north end, the Palais du Luxembourg, the 1627 palace of Maria de Medici, is now used by the French Senate. Rather austere from the outside, its elaborate interior features temporary art exhibitions and a Delacroix painting in the library. *Address:* enter off rue de Vaugirard (north), rue Auguste Comte (south), boulevard St-Michel (east), or rue Guynemer (west). *Métro:* Luxembourg (B). *Buses:* 21, 38, 58, 82, 83, 84, 89. *Admission:* Free for park, with fees for pony rides, tennis courts, and marionette shows. On Sunday, free tours of the Senate and palace are available from 10am-11am and 2:30pm-3:30pm (you must show your passport).

Musée de Minéralogie

Housed in the 1815 Hôtel de Vendôme and School of Advanced Mining Engineering, this museum has one of the largest collections in the world about mining. Exhibits include documents, hardware, and instruments concerning the mining industry in France and Europe. *Address:* 60 boulevard St-Michel (phone 40-51-91-39). *Hours:* Sat 10am-12:30pm & 2pm-5pm; Tue-Fri 1:30pm-6pm. *Métro:* Luxembourg (B). *Buses:* 21, 27, 38, 82, 84, 85, 89. *Admission:* 20F.

Musée Moissan

Ferdinand-Frédéric-Henri Moissan was a renowned French pharmacist and winner of the Nobel Prize for chemistry in 1906. A small museum, housed in the Université Paris V phar-

The grotto-like Fontaine de Medicis is part of the Jardin du Luxembourg.

macy school building, presents the most important aspects of his scientific work (1852-1907) through photographs, documents, and scientific instruments. *Address:* 4 avenue de l'Observatoire (phone 43-29-12-08). *Hours:* open by appointment only; closed August. *Métro:* Luxembourg (B), Port Royal (B). *Buses:* 38, 58, 82, 83, 91.

Closerie des Lilas & Marshall Ney Monument

While you enjoy coffee on the outdoor terrace of the Closerie des Lilas, a restaurant popular with Hemingway and other literary greats, take a look at the sword-waving statue honoring Marshall Ney, one of Napoléon's favorite generals. A royalist firing squad executed Ney here in 1815. *Address:* corner of boulevard Montparnasse and avenue de l'Observatoire. *Métro:* Port Royal (B). *Buses:* 38, 83, 91.

Musée Édouard Branly

The electric wave detector and other instruments used in the experiments of physicist Édouard Branly, the inventor of wireless telegraphy, are displayed in this small museum. *Address:* 21 rue d'Assas, in the Institute Catholique de Paris (phone 49-54-52-00). *Hours:* open by appointment only. *Métro:* Rennes (12). *Buses:* 48, 58, 68, 83, 89, 94, 95, 96.

Musée de Bible et Terre Sainte

Objects and ceramics from Palestine dating from 5,000 BC to 600 AD are displayed in this small museum housed in the Institute Catholique de Paris. *Address:* 21 rue d'Assas (phone 44-39-52-00). *Hours:* Sat 3pm-6pm. *Métro/Buses:* same as Musée Edouard Branly.

Musée Zadkine

Set back from the street via a narrow alley, a museum and garden exhibit the works of Russian sculptor Ossip Zadkine, who was heavily influenced by Cubism. A Paris resident since 1909, he worked from this location from 1928 until his death in 1967. His sculpture is found all over Paris and Europe. *Address:* 100 bis rue d'Assas (phone 43-26-91-90). *Hours:* Tue-Sun 10am-5:30pm. *Métro:* Port-Royal (B), Vavin (4). *Buses:* 82, 83. *Admission:* 17.5F, Carte Musées et Monuments.

Tati

Always crowded with shoppers, often elbow-to-elbow, this store is a must for bargain hunters and a wild shopping experience. Prices for new clothes (shirts from 5F, dresses from 30F), fabrics, and decorative items are extremely cheap. But don't go here if you're claustrophobic—it may take you hours to push your way back out. *Address:* 140 rue de Rennes. *Hours:* Mon-Sat 9:30am-7pm. *Métro:* St-Placide (4). *Buses:* 48, 89, 94, 95.

Poîlane

Lionel Poîlane, a.k.a. *Le Roi du Pain* (The King of Bread), is the most famous baker in France. If you compare his creations against other bakeries, you'll notice a big difference in texture and taste. His shop stocks the standard *baguette* (extremely cheap), plus other types of bread made from a variety of ingredients. *Address:* 8 rue du Cherche-Midi (phone 45-48-42-59).

Hours: Mon-Sat 7am-8pm. *Métro:* Sèvres-Babylone (10, 12), St-Sulpice (4). *Buses:* 70, 75.

Musée Ernest Hébert

The paintings of artist Ernest Hébert (1817-1908) and his personal art collection are displayed in the mansion Hôtel de Montmorency. *Address:* 85 rue du Cherche-Midi (phone 42-22-23-82). *Hours:* Mon & Wed-Fri 12:30pm-6pm; Sat, Sun, holidays 2pm-6pm. *Métro:* Vaneau (10). *Buses:* 28, 39, 70, 82, 89, 91, 92, 94, 95, 96. *Admission:* 15, Carte Musées et Monuments.

The Tour Eiffel viewed from the Parc du Champ de Mars.

7th Arrondissement

The most upscale residential district on the south side of the Seine River, the 7th arrondissement is also home to the Tour Eiffel, the city's most famous landmark. Amongst the schools, government buildings, and foreign embassies in this attractive area, there are chic shops and restaurants, long promenades, and several outstanding museums—from the lovely Musée Rodin to the massive Musée de l'Armée.

The boundaries of the 7th arrondissement are triangular: Seine River (north), place Henri Queuille (where east and west intersect), rues de Sèvres and des Sts-Père (east), and boulevard de Suffren (west).

Tour Eiffel

The 1,266-foot high Tour Eiffel—the universal symbol of Paris—remains the city's most-visited sight. Consisting of 12,000 steel sections and 2.5 million rivets, it was built for the World's Fair in 1889 by engineer Gustave Eiffel. On clear days, you can get marvelous views of Paris from its lofty platforms. *Address:* between quai du Branly and avenue Gustave Eiffel (phone 44-11-23-45). *Hours:* summer: Mon-Sun 9am-midnight; winter: Mon-Sun 9:30am-11pm. *Métro:* Bir-Hakeim (6), École Militaire (8), Champ de Mars/Tour Eiffel (C). *Buses:* 42, 69, 72, 80, 82, 87, 92. *Admission:* to the first platform by elevator, 20F; to the first and second platforms via the stairs, 14F. The third platform (accessible only by elevator) and restaurants are expensive. A free movie discussing the tower's construction is shown at the first stage from 10am to 7:30pm daily.

Office du Tourisme: Bureau Tour Eiffel

This small branch of the Office du Tourisme has lots of free maps and literature about Paris's sights. *Address:* Champ de Mars (phone 45-51-22-15). *Hours:* May 1-Sep 30: daily 11am-6pm. *Métro/Buses:* same as Tour Eiffel.

Parc du Champ de Mars

This former military parade ground, which stretches from the Tour Eiffel to the École Militaire, offers one of the best places to view the tower. As the longest open space of grass in the city, it serves as the site of neighborhood festivals and free outdoor concerts during the summer. Smaller side parks with benches and play areas for children border both sides, and there are terraced ponds and paths beneath the tower. *Address:* between avenue de la Motte-Piquet and Tour Eiffel, crisscrossed by numerous streets. *Métro/Buses:* same as Tour Eiffel.

École Militaire

The large group of neoclassical buildings opposite the south end of the Parc du Champ de Mars is the École Militaire (French Military Academy). Constructed from 1751 to 1782, it began as a school for army officers; Napoléon Bonaparte is its most famous graduate. Unfortunately, you can't get inside for a tour unless you have written permission from the Commandant. But since you'll be in the area viewing the Tour Eiffel, take a look at the school's exterior and imagine Napoléon coming through the gate on his horse. On the other side, peek through the gates at place de Fontenay for a glimpse of the gardens in the parade ground. *Address:* 43 avenue de la Motte-Piquet and place de Fontenay. *Métro:* École Militaire (8). *Buses:* 28, 49, 80, 82, 87, 92.

Maison de l'UNESCO

The United Nations Education, Scientific, & Cultural Organization (UNESCO) features unique modern buildings (one is Y-shaped on piles, and another has fluted concrete walls with an accordion-pleated roof) and a great collection of art. On its grounds are sculpture by Calder and Moore, plus a Noguchi-designed garden. Inside, there are Picasso paintings, Lurçat and Le Corbusier tapestries, painted walls by Miró, an Arp sculptured relief, and works by other lesser-known international artists. *Address:* 7 place de Fontenoy (phone 45-68-10-00). *Hours:* Mon-Fri 9am-12:30pm & 2:30pm-6pm. *Métro:* Segur (10). *Buses:* 49. *Admission:* free; however, you might need permission to enter, depending on the level of security required for current seminars and meetings. Call in advance.

Musée Valentin Haüy

This small museum features appliances and devices used to

teach the blind. It's dedicated to Valentin Haüy (1745-1822), who invented some of these devices. *Address:* 5 rue Duroc (phone 44-49-27-27). *Hours:* Tue & Wed 2:30pm-5pm; closed August. *Métro:* Duroc (10, 13). *Buses:* 28, 70, 87, 92.

Hôtel des Invalides

The large, quadrilateral Hôtel des Invalides with a partial moat was designed by Libéral Bruant in 1671 as a home for wounded soldiers. (A portion is still used as a veteran's hospital.) Considered a masterpiece of 17th-century architecture, the structure today contains some of the city's best sights and museums, including the Église du Dome with its shiny gold dome, the Église St-Louis, Napléon's tomb, and four museums: Musée de l'Armée, Musée d'Histoire Contemporaine, Musée de l'Ordre de la Liberation, and Musée de Plans et Reliefs. The Jardin de l'Intendant near the south entrance is a pretty setting with good views of the Tour Eiffel stretching above the townhouses. *Address:* see specifics below.

Musée de l'Armée

You'll need several hours to see even a small portion of the Musée de l'Armée. The largest army museum in France, it offers an exhaustive collection—over 40,000 exhibits spread over several floors of the Hôtel des Invalides. It includes emblems, uniforms, weapons (from swords to automatic rifles), suits of armor, battle flags, personal items of Napoléon (including his dog [stuffed]), models illustrating battles, and other military equipment. *Address:* enter at place des Invalides (north) or place Vauban (south) (phone 44-42-37-72). *Hours:* Oct 1-March 31: daily 10am-5pm; April 1-Sep 30: 10am-6pm; closed Jan 1, May 1, Nov 1, Dec 25. *Métro:* Invalides (8, 13, C), Latour-Maubourg (8), École Militaire (8), Varenne (13), St-François-Xavier (13). *Buses:* 28, 49, 63, 69, 82, 83, 87, 92. *Admission:* The 35F ticket is an extremely cheap bargain. It's valid for two consecutive days and gives you entry to this museum, plus the Tomb of Napoléon, Église St-Louis, and Musée des Plans et Reliefs. Carte Musées et Monuments also valid.

Tomb of Napoléon & Église du Dôme

The large, rusty-red porphyry sarcophagus containing Napoléon's body is set in a circular crypt cut into the floor of the Église du Dome so that tourists can view but not touch. The

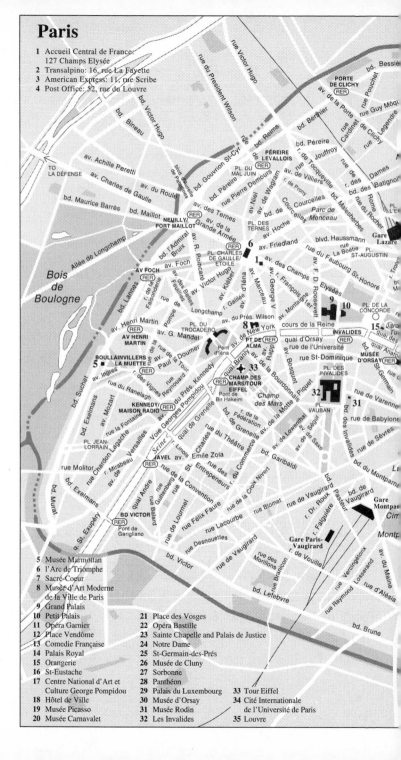

Paris

1 Accueil Central de France:
  127 Champs Elysée
2 Transalpino: 16, rue La Fayette
3 American Express: 11, rue Scribe
4 Post Office: 52, rue du Louvre

5 Musée Marmottan
6 l'Arc de Triomphe
7 Sacré-Coeur
8 Musée d'Art Moderne
  de la Ville de Paris
9 Grand Palais
10 Petit Palais
11 Opéra Garnier
12 Place Vendôme
13 Comedie Française
14 Palais Royal
15 Orangerie
16 St-Eustache
17 Centre National d'Art et
   Culture George Pompidou
18 Hôtel de Ville
19 Musée Picasso
20 Musée Carnavalet

21 Place des Vosges
22 Opéra Bastille
23 Sainte Chapelle and Palais de Justice
24 Notre Dame
25 St-Germain-des-Prés
26 Musée de Cluny
27 Sorbonne
28 Panthéon
29 Palais du Luxembourg
30 Musée d'Orsay
31 Musée Rodin
32 Les Invalides

33 Tour Eiffel
34 Cité Internationale
   de l'Université de Paris
35 Louvre

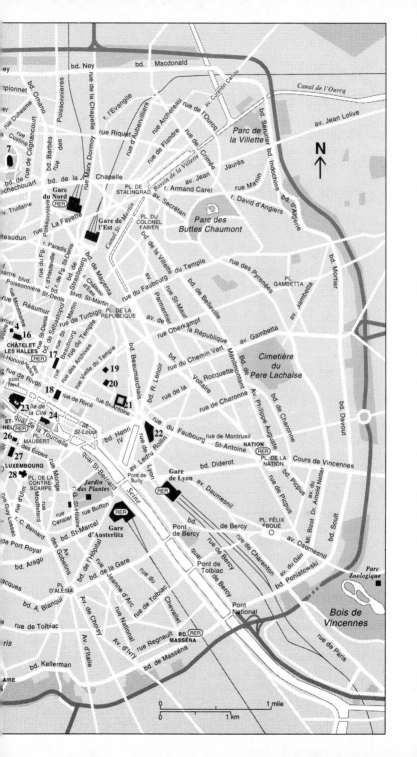

bas-reliefs carved in the crypt walls depict institutions founded by Napoléon, and the 12 angel statues surrounding the tomb symbolize his military campaigns. Napoléon shares the building with the tombs of his brothers Joseph and Jerome, three of his generals, and World War I hero Marshal Foch. *Address:* immediate entry from place Vauban. *Hours/Métro/Buses/ Admission:* same as Musée de l'Armée.

Musée des Plans et Reliefs
This museum, an extension of the Musée de l'Armée, has hundreds of plans and models of 17th- and 18th-century fortified towns and cities in France and abroad. *Address/Hours/ Métro/ Buses/Admission:* same as Musée de l'Armée.

Église St-Louis-des-Invalides
The smaller of the two churches in the Hôtel des Invalides is decorated with captured enemy flags and banners from past military campaigns. It also contains the tombs of Generals Joffre, Leclerc, Giraud, and Juin. *Address/Hours/Métro/Buses/ Admission:* same as Musée de l'Armée.

Musée de l'Ordre de la Libération
The Order of Liberation, created by de Gaulle after the fall of France in 1940, honors soldiers and civilians who made significant contributions to the Allied victory in World War II. The museum, in a small section of the Hôtel des Invalides, has over 200 cabinets displaying episodes of the war in France. *Address:* 51 bis boulevard de La Tour-Maubourg (phone 47-05-04-10). *Hours:* Mon-Sat 2pm-5pm; closed May 1, June 17, Nov 1, Dec 25. *Métro:* La Tour-Maubourg (8). *Buses:* 28, 49, 67, 69, 89, 92.

Institut Autrichien
The Austrian cultural institute has free lectures, concerts, and an occasional art exhibition. *Address:* 30 boulevard des Invalides (phone 45-05-27-10). *Hours:* Mon-Sat 9am-evening (depends on the event). *Métro:* St-François-Xavier (13). *Buses:* 28, 87.

Faubourg St-Germain
The neighborhood between the Hôtel Invalides and the 6th arrondissement was Paris's most fashionable residential area in the 18th century. The mansions today are used by French ministries, foreign embassies, and very wealthy families. Except for

the Musée Auguste Rodin (see below), they are open by invitation only, so you'll have to settle for viewing them from the street. The best buildings are on the east-west rues Varenne, de Lille, St-Dominique, de l'Université, and de Grenelle. *Address:* approximate boundaries are Seine River (north), rue de Babylone (south), rue du Bac and boulevard Raspail (east), and boulevard des Invalides and rue de Constantine (west). *Métro:* Varenne (13), Invalides (8, 13, C), Assemblée Nationale, Solférino, Rue du Bac (12). *Buses:* 69, 87.

Musée Auguste Rodin

This is one of the prettiest museum settings in Paris. Set in a spacious and quiet park filled with flowers, trees, a central fountain, and statues, the 16-room Hôtel Biron—the former residence (1904-17) of France's most famous sculptor—is now a superb showcase for his major achievements. Three of Rodin's most famous bronzes—*The Thinker, Burghers of Calais*, and *Gates of Hell*—are near the entrance. Inside the mansion, you'll enjoy more sculpture, plus exhibits of Rodin's letters, drawings, paintings, furniture, personal art collection, and other memorabilia. *Address:* 77 rue de Varenne (phone 44-18-61-10). *Hours:* April 1-Sep 30: Tue-Sun 9:30am-5:45pm; Oct 1-March 31: Tue-Sun 9:30am-4:45pm; closed Jan 1, May 1, Dec 25. *Métro:* Invalides (C), Varenne (13). *Buses:* 28, 49, 69, 82, 92. *Admission:* Carte Musées et Monuments, 5F for sculpture garden only.

Musée Anatomie Delmas-Orfila-Rouviere

This museum displays 5,800 anatomical items, from the real thing to molds of organs and body parts. Not for the squeamish! *Address:* 45 rue des St-Pères in the Paris V René Descartes University (phone 42-86-20-47). *Hours:* by appointment. *Métro:* St-Germain-des-Prés (4). *Buses:* 39, 48, 63, 84, 86, 87, 95.

Palais Bourbon & Assemblée Nationale

Inside the colonnaded Palais Bourbon, a Classically-inspired 18th-century mansion, is the meeting hall for the *Assemblée Nationale* (the main governing body in France) and the official residence of the organization's President. The public is allowed to attend the sessions and tour the lavish palace, which features a Delacroix painting on the ceiling in the library. *Address:* 33 quai d'Orsay (phone 40-63-60-00). *Hours:* Mon-Fri 9am-11am

& 2pm-4pm. In session April-June & Oct-Dec; call in advance for exact times. *Métro:* Assemblée Nationale (12), Invalides (8,13, C). *Buses:* 24, 63, 83, 84, 94. *Admission:* free with advance authorization in writing. (Bring your passport for ID.)

Basilique Ste-Clotilde

Set on a pretty square in the heart of the 7th arrondissement's government district, this 19th-century, neo-Gothic church was built by German architect F.C. Gau. It features a few walls painted by Pradier, reliefs about its namesake, and tall twin towers. *Address:* 23 bis rue Las-Cases. *Métro:* Solférino (12). *Buses:* 69.

Centre Culturel Canadien

The well-funded Canadian cultural center offers free art exhibitions, concerts, films, and videos, plus an excellent library and music reference room. *Address:* 5 rue de Constantine (phone 45-51-35-73; call 45-51-35-41 for taped message about daily events). *Hours:* Mon-Fri 10am-7pm (open later for some events). *Métro:* Invalides (8, 13, C). *Buses:* 63, 69.

Centre Culturel Britannique & British Institute

Free concerts, films, and lectures are held here often, plus you may use its library to sample current British newspapers, books, and records. *Address:* 9-11 rue de Constantine (phone 49-55-73-00). *Hours:* Mon-Fri 10am-evening (depending on the event). *Métro/Buses:* same as Centre Culturel Canadien.

Institut Neederlandais

This active cultural organization presents free exhibitions of contemporary art, plus occasional concerts of jazz, classical, and contemporary music from the Netherlands. *Address:* 121 rue Lille (phone 47-05-85-99). *Hours:* Tue-Sun 1pm-7pm. *Métro:* Assemblée Nationale (12). *Buses:* 63, 68, 69.

Galerie Adrien Maeght

For decades, this has been one of the most progressive art galleries in Paris. Its owner discovered Calder, Miró, and Giacometti. *Address:* 42-46 rue du Bac (phone 45-48-45-15). *Hours:* Mon-Sat 10:30am-1pm & 2pm-6:30pm. *Métro:* rue du Bac (12). *Buses:* 63, 68, 69.

Musée d'Orsay

One of the city's most important collections of French sculpture, photography, and decorative art is housed on several floors of a beautifully refurbished train station (with wide open spaces, tall ceilings, and lots of glass). The museum's enormous collection, spanning 1850-1914, includes the great Impressionist paintings formerly seen in the *Jeu de Paume* and some of the best early modern art owned by France. Other schools of art, including the Symbolists, Neo- and Post-Impressionists, and Art Nouveau, are well represented.

Besides the permanent collection, the Musée d'Orsay offers temporary exhibitions focusing on specific artists. Like the Louvre, this art museum requires several hours to see properly. Get a free museum map with your ticket and choose your highlights. *Address:* 1 rue de Bellechasse (phone 40-49-48-14). *Hours:* June 20-Sep 20: Tue, Wed, Fri-Sun 9am-6pm, Thur 9am-9:45pm; Sept 21-June 19: Tue, Wed, Fri 10am-6pm, Thur 10am-9:45pm; Sun 9am-6pm; closed Jan 1, May 1, Dec 25. *Métro:* Solferino (12), Musée d'Orsay (C). *Buses:* 24, 63, 68, 69, 73, 83, 84, 94. *Admission:* Carte Musées et Monuments.

Musée de la Légion d'Honneur et des Ordres de Chevalerie

In the 1878 Hôtel de Salm, across the street from the Musée d'Orsay, a small museum details the history of the most prestigious civilian order in France. Museum highlights include displays of French and foreign medals, uniforms, swords, and paintings by Van Loo. *Address:* 2 rue de Bellechasse (phone 45-55-95-16). *Hours:* Tue-Sun 2pm-5pm. *Métro/Buses:* same as Musée d'Orsay. *Admission:* Carte Musées et Monuments.

Debauve & Gallais

Delicious chocolates and other confectionery creations have been made in the kitchens of this old shop—which is also an architectural treasure worth seeing—since 1819. If your sweet tooth is demanding, satisfy it here. (Somehow, our resistance is always low when we're near this store.) Otherwise, pause to drool at the window for a minute and catch the delectable smells seeping out the door. *Address:* 30 rue des Saints-Pères. *Hours:* Tue-Sat 10am-7pm; closed August. *Métro:* St-Germain-des-Prés (4). *Buses:* 39, 48, 63, 84, 86, 87, 95.

Bibliothèque-Musée de la Société de l'Histoire du Protestantisme Français

This museum and library offers books, engravings, and manuscripts concerning the history of the Protestant church in France. *Address:* 54 rue des Saints-Pères (phone 45-48-62-07). *Hours:* Tue-Sat by appointment only; closed Easter week and Aug 1-Sept 15. *Métro/ Buses:* same as Debauve & Gallais.

American Church

Operated by Americans for several decades, this church has services in English and free events every month. They also have a bulletin board listing jobs, apartments, and other needs for longer stays in Paris. *Address:* 65 quai d'Orsay (phone 47-05-07-99). *Hours:* 9am-evening (depending on the event). *Métro:* Pont de l'Alma (C). *Buses:* 63, 80, 92.

Musée des Égouts

One of the most offbeat ways to see Paris is to explore its sewers. This small exhibition space explains the water cycle of Paris, the components of the sewers, and their history. On the tour, note the pneumatic tubes that were used by the postal service to transport mail until 1984. Resistance fighters used the maze of tunnels, constructed under Napoléon III, as escape routes during the Nazi occupation. *Address:* place de la Resistance at quai d'Orsay (phone 47-05-10-29) *Hours:* Sat-Wed 11am-5pm; closed after heavy rains and the last three weeks of Jan. *Métro:* Alma-Marceau (9), Pont de l'Alma (C). *Buses:* 42, 63, 80, 92. *Admission:* Carte Musées et Monuments.

Centre Culturel de Mexique

The cultural center of Mexico offers a variety of free concerts, art exhibitions, and other events. *Address:* 28 boulevard Raspail (phone 45-49-16-26). *Hours:* Mon-Fri 10am-6pm, Sat 2pm-7pm. *Métro/Buses:* same as Au Bon Marché.

Fondation Jean Dubuffet

Temporary art exhibitions concerning the revolutionary modern artist and writer are shown here. A research library provides more insight into the art of Dubuffet, who became an artist in his mid-40's after being a successful wine merchant. *Address:* 137 rue Sèvres (phone 47-34-12-63). *Hours:* Mon-Fri 2pm-6pm. *Métro:* Duroc (10, 13). *Buses:* 39, 70, 89.

8th Arrondissement

The elegant 8th arrondissement is dominated by the avenue des Champs-Élysées. While it's easy to stay busy visiting the various sights along this great avenue—place de la Concorde, the Arc de Triomphe, Petit Palais, and numerous stores and cafés—there are excellent sights throughout the arrondissement, including the small Parc de Monceau on its north end, the classically-designed Madeleine church, several small art museums, and the couture houses of the world's top designers.

The 8th arrondissement's boundaries are boulevards Courcelles and des Batignolles (north), Seine River (south), place de la Concorde and de la Madeleine, and rues Royale, Vignon, Tronchet, du Havre, and d'Amsterdam (east), and place de Charles-de-Gaulle and avenues Wagram and Marceau (west).

Avenue des Champs-Élysées

Although this famed ten-lane avenue is always crowded with tourists, it's still a great and sometimes amusing journey (Americans will chuckle ruefully at the proliferation of U.S. businesses and goods) to walk its entire 1.25-mile length from the Arc de Triomphe to place de la Concorde. Other sights along the avenue or nearby are listed below. *Métro:* Charles de Gaulle-Étoile (1, 2, 6, A), George V (1), Franklin D. Roosevelt (1, 9), Champs-Élysées/Clemenceau (1, 13), Concorde (1, 8, 12). *Buses:* 22, 28, 30, 31, 42, 49, 52, 71, 73, 80, 83, 92.

Arc de Triomphe

After the Tour Eiffel, the Arc de Triomphe is the most-recognized monument in Paris. The huge arch, 164 feet high, towering over place Charles-de-Gaulle at the west end of avenue des Champs-Élysées, was built by order of Napoléon as homage to his armies. Since its completion in 1836, it has been the site of much history and adventure, as invaders have marched past it and an occasional pilot on a dare will fly through it. At the monument's ground level, take a good look at the carvings of soldiers and other figures, the tomb of France's Unknown Soldier with an eternal flame (there's a re-lighting ceremony every evening at 6:30pm), and the cars frantically circling the monument in search of one of 12 streets that flow into the circular place. For a better look at this congested area, avenue des Champs-Élysées, and other Paris sights, go to the top of the arch, where you'll find a museum explaining its history. *Address:* place Charles-de-Gaulle (phone 43-80-31-31). To reach the Arc, enter the tunnel that goes beneath the place from the north corner of avenue des Champs-Élysées to avenue de Grande Armée. Unless you have a death wish, do not attempt to cross the traffic circle on foot! *Hours:* April 1-Sep 30: daily 10am-5:30pm; Oct 1-Nov 11 & Feb 1-March 31: 10am-5pm; Nov 12-Jan 31: 10am-4:30pm; closed for occasional special ceremonies. *Métro:* Charles de Gaulle-Étoile (1, 2, 6, A). *Buses:* 22, 30, 31, 52, 71, 73, 92, Air France. *Admission:* free at ground level, Carte Musées et Monuments for admission to the museum and top of the arch.

Office du Tourisme et des Congrés de Paris: Bureau d'Accueil Central

Opposite the Arc de Triomphe, at the headquarters of the Paris tourist information and convention bureau, you can get tons of free maps and literature about Paris. Ask for the current events magazine *Paris Selection, Time Out,* and the *Paris User's Guide,* a 200-page paperback book in French and English with information about sights and attractions for both tourists and business people. *Address:* 127 avenue des Champs-Élysées (phone 49-52-53-53). *Hours:* daily 9am-8pm; closed Jan 1, May 1, Dec 25. *Métro/Buses:* same as Arc de Triomphe.

Virgin Megastore

Halfway down the avenue des Champs-Élysées from the Arc, the biggest music store in Paris lets you sample and browse through the latest in international music and gawk at a trendy crowd. *Address:* 52-60 avenue des Champs-Élysées (phone 49-53-50-00). *Hours:* Sun 2pm-midnight; Mon-Thur 10am-midnight; Fri & Sat 10am-1am. *Métro:* Franklin D. Roosevelt (1, 9). *Buses:* 32, 42, 43, 49, 73, 80, 93.

Lido Cabaret Normandie

It certainly doesn't fit the budget of this book, but if you're curious while taking your avenue des Champs-Élysées stroll, check out the famed nightclub's current posters and save your money. The show itself will set you back at least $85 ($130 with dinner), with drinks as high as 175F. *Address:* 116 bis avenue des Champs-Élysées. *Métro:* George V (1, 9). *Buses:* 73.

Église Danoise

This small Danish church on a street behind the Lido offers regular free classical music concerts of Danish and Nordic composers. *Address:* 17 rue Lord-Byron. *Métro:* George V (1, 9), Charles de Gaulle-Étoile (1, 2, 6, A). *Buses:* 52, 73.

Cathédrale Americain

Although Paris abounds in Catholic churches, this is one of the few offering mass in English. A service was held here in 1905 for American Revolutionary War hero John Paul Jones, who was buried in Paris. After the service, his casket was sent to Annapolis. *Address:* 23 avenue George V (phone 47-20-17-92). *Métro:* Alma Marceau (9), George V (1, 9). *Buses:* 32, 92.

Institut Géographique National (IGN)

The IGN, like America's National Geographic Society, funds international expeditions and creates a wide range of publications about geographic topics. Their retail store stocks a good supply of travel books, GR hiking route guides, maps, photographs of Paris, day packs, and other travel paraphernalia. For veteran travelers and explorers, it's fun to browse (but you'll need willpower!). *Address:* 107 rue La Boétie. *Hours:* Mon-Fri 8am-6:50pm, Sat 10am-12:30pm & 1:45pm-5:20pm. *Métro:* Franklin D. Roosevelt (1, 9). *Buses:* 28, 32, 73, 52, 80, 83, 93.

Marché aux Timbres et Aux Pins

A favorite among collectors, this active outdoor market sells a large assortment of old stamps, postcards, télecartes (the hottest collectible in France due to the colorful images printed on them), and decorative pins like those sold at the Olympics and other events. Many of the items are extremely cheap. *Address:* in park along avenue Gabriel between avenue Marigny and avenue Matignon. *Hours:* Thur, Sat, & Sun 10am-dusk. *Métro:* Franklin D. Roosevelt (1, 9). *Buses:* 52, 73, 83.

Marionettes des Champs-Élysées

Classic marionette theater with Punch and Judy is performed in the same park as the Marché aux Timbres. *Address/Métro/Buses:* same as Marché aux Timbres. *Hours:* one-hour performances on Wed, Sat, & Sun at 3pm, 4pm, & 5pm. *Admission:* 12.50F.

Avenue Montaigne

Hang onto your wallet! This wide avenue is home to chic boutiques and showrooms of the fashion designers Christian Dior (#30), Céline (#38), Chanel (#42), Guy Laroche (#29), Nina Ricci (#39), Thiery Mugler (#34), Ungaro (#2), and Valentino (#17-19). The only way you'll stay within the "extremely cheap" guidelines is by window-shopping. *Address:* between Rond Point des Champs-Élysées and place de l'Alma. *Métro:* Franklin D. Roosevelt (1, 9), Alma Marceau (9). *Buses:* 42, 80.

Maison de la Vigne et du Vin du France

The headquarters of the French wine industry has exhibits of old bottles, maps, and information about wine-making. *Address:* 21 rue François-1er (phone 47-20-20-76). *Hours:* Mon-Fri 10am-6pm. *Métro:* Franklin D. Roosevelt (1, 9). *Buses:* 32, 42, 73, 80.

Grand Palais and Fondation Lartigue

The neo-Baroque Grand Palais, with its magnificent glass and steel dome, and the Petit Palais (see below) across the street were built for the 1900 World Exhibition. Divided into several galleries, the Grand Palais hosts major art exhibitions, ranging from retrospectives of top artists to thematic shows. Also in the building is the gallery of the Fondation Lartigue, which oversees photographs donated to France by Jacques-Henri Lartigue, who chronicled Paris during the early 20th century. *Address:* avenue Winston-Churchill (phone 42-89-54-10) *Hours:* Wed 10am-10pm & Thur-Mon 10am-8pm; closed Jan 1, May 1, Dec 25. *Métro:* Champs-Élysées/Clemenceau (1, 13). *Buses:* 28, 42, 49, 72, 73, 83. *Admission:* 20F for Lartigue gallery, free-40F for art exhibitions.

Musée du Petit Palais

Often bypassed by tourists en route to the Musées Louvre and d'Orsay, this museum has one of the best collections in the city, with paintings by Sisley, Boudin, Monet, Gauguin, Degas, Delacroix, Géricault, Cézanne, Bonnard, Courbet, Cranach, Rembrandt, Rubens, and many other outstanding 15th-19th century artists. Temporary exhibitions of renowned painters are held here regularly. *Address:* avenue Winston-Churchill (phone 42-65-12-73). *Hours:* Tue-Sun 10am-5:40pm. *Métro:* same as Grand Palais. *Admission:* Carte Musées et Monuments.

Pont Alexandre III
The most photographed bridge in Paris is the Pont Alexandre III. The congested, multi-lane span, built for the 1900 World's Fair, is adorned with sculptures of cherubs, ornate Belle Epoque lanterns, and monumental pedestals at its entrances, which are topped with gilded sculptures of winged horses. *Address:* cours de la Reine to quai d'Orsay. *Métro:* Invalides (8, 13, C). *Buses:* 72, 83, 93.

Palais de la Découverte
Built in 1937 behind the Grand Palais for the International Exhibition of Arts and Techniques, this science museum offers a great planetarium. Although it has been displaced by the new science and industry museum at La Villette (see 19th arrondissement), this one is much cheaper. *Address:* avenue Franklin-D.-Roosevelt (phone 40-74-80-00). *Hours:* Tue-Sat 9:30am-6pm & Sun 10am-7pm. *Métro:* Champs-Élysées Clemenceau (1, 13), Franklin-D.-Roosevelt (1, 9). *Buses:* 24, 28, 42, 43, 49, 84, 94. *Admission:* 15F for planetarium only; free movies on science and nature subjects.

Place de la Concorde
The busy traffic intersection on the east end of the avenue des Champs-Élysées marks the site of 1,343 executions by guillotine during the French Revolution, as well as a tank battle during the Liberation of Paris in 1944. In the middle of the square is the Luxor Obelisk, a 75-foot-high pink granite column presented to Charles X by the Viceroy of Egypt in 1829. The obelisk is flanked on both sides by spraying fountains and large statues along the place's perimeter. Be very careful crossing for a close-up of the obelisk—there are no crosswalks or lights. *Métro:* Concorde (1, 8, 12). *Buses:* 24, 42, 52, 72, 73, 84, 94.

Église de la Madeleine

A few blocks off place de la Concorde, the Église de la Madeleine has become a Paris landmark because of its impressive façade resembling a Greek temple. Completed in 1842, it features 52 fluted Corinthian columns that circle the entire building. Go inside to view its altar, the marble inlay work in the walls, and the statues, including the *Baptism of Jesus* by Rude. The church has great acoustics, and the free classical music concerts regularly held here are a delight. Also, from its elevated entrance, you'll get good views down rue Royale to place de la Concorde and the Hôtel des Invalides in the distance. *Address:* middle of place de la Madeleine. *Métro:* Madeleine (8, 12), Concorde (1, 8, 12). *Buses:* 24, 42, 52, 84, 94.

Kiosque-Théâtre

The small ticket stand on the west side of the Église de la Madeleine sells theater tickets at half-price on the day of the show. *Address:* 15 place de la Madeleine. *Hours:* Tue-Sat 12:30pm-8pm & Sun 12:30pm-4pm. *Métro/Buses:* same as Église de la Madeleine.

Fauchon

Opposite the Église de la Madeleine is the gourmet food emporium Fauchon. With all the smells and interesting food displays, it takes a lot of willpower just to browse here (there are over 20,000 products), so lock your wallet as you enter. Fauchon's self-service cafeteria across the street gives you a chance to sample some of the wares. *Address:* place de la Madeleine at rue de Sèze. *Hours:* Mon-Sat 9:40am-6:30pm. *Métro/Buses:* same as Église de la Madeleine.

Rue du Faubourg-St-Honoré

The couture houses and boutiques of some of the world's greatest fashion designers line this long street, and you'll occasionally glimpse models leaving the houses in the latest garb. The stores are free for window-shopping and browsing inside, though if you're not already dressed to the hilt, you may get some glares from the sales clerks. Pierre Cardin (#82), Gucci (#2), Ashida (#34), Chloé (#60), Louis Feraud (#88), Grés (#17-21), Hermès (#24), Christian Lacroix (#73), Karl Lagerfield (#19), Lanvin (#15), Sonia Rykiel (#70), and Yves St-Laurent

(#38) are the most famous on this street. Two notable non-fashion shops on the street are Dalloyau (#99-101) and La Maison du Chocolate (#225). Both sell some of the most luscious chocolates and pastries you'll find anywhere in the world. (Hey, one pastry won't kill your budget!) The high-walled building at the corner of avenue de Marigny with lots of police guarding its entrance is the Palais de l'Élysées, the official residence of the President of France. It is open one day each year to French citizens. *Address:* between place des Ternes and rue Royale. *Métro:* Madeleine (8, 12), St-Philippe-du-Roule (9), Ternes (2). *Buses:* 24, 38, 49, 52, 80, 83.

Église St-Michael
This Anglican church has three weekly services in English and offers free concerts and music recitals throughout the year. *Address:* 5 rue d'Aguesseau (phone 47-42-70-88). *Hours:* services Thur 12:45pm & Sun 10:30am & 6:30pm. *Métro:* Madeleine (8, 12). *Buses:* 52.

Église St-Philippe-du-Roule
Free classical music concerts are held in this 18th-century church, which resembles a Roman building with a four-columned entrance. *Address:* 154 rue du Faubourg-St-Honoré. *Métro:* St-Philippe du Roule (9). *Buses:* 28, 32, 52, 80, 83, 93.

Église St-Alexandre-Nevsky
For something completely different, go see the largest Russian Orthodox church in Paris, easily recognizable by its six golden onion domes. Inside, it has paintings, sculpture, and religious icons. *Address:* 12 rue Daru. *Métro:* Courcelles (2), Ternes (2). *Buses:* 30, 43, 84, 93.

Parc de Monceau
The Parc de Monceau is the prettiest small park in Paris. Set in an upper-crust neighborhood, it is patterned after the English garden parks of the 18th century, combined with some unique sights: a miniature pyramid, ancient columns in a pond, and a small rotunda (Chartres Pavilion) used as a tollhouse in the 18th-century city wall. *Address:* main entrance off boulevard de Courcelles; other entrances via avenues Hoche, Rysdaël, or Vélasquez. *Métro:* Monceau (2). *Buses:* 30, 94.

Musée Nissim de Camondo

On the southeast corner of Parc Monceau, housed in a mansion patterned after Versailles' Petit Trianon, this museum features one of the city's best collections of decorative arts from the second half of the 18th century. *Address:* 63 rue de Monceau, (phone 45-63-26-32). *Hours:* Wed-Sun 10am-5pm; closed Jan 1, May 1, Dec 25. *Métro:* Monceau (2). *Buses:* 30, 84, 94. *Admission:* Carte Musées et Monuments.

Musée Cernuschi

Next to the above museum, the Musée Cernuschi displays an excellent collection of Asian art. Its exhibits include silk paintings, ceramics, Buddha statuettes, and funeral statuary from the 3rd to 20th centuries. *Address:* 7 avenue Vélasquez (phone 45-63-50-75). *Hours:* Tue-Sun 10am-5:40pm. *Métro/Buses:* same as Musée Nissim de Camondo. *Admission:* 17.5F, Carte Musées et Monuments.

Gare St-Lazare

On the border of the 9th arrondissement, the most famous train station in Paris has been immortalized in paintings by Monet and was the site of Cartier-Bresson's famous photograph of a man leaping across a puddle. Located near the center of north Paris, it's a major demarcation point for public buses, suburban rail lines, and for rail travel to Normandy and northwest France. Two sculptures by Arman depicting time (stacked watches) and luggage decorate its main entrance. *Address:* cour de Rome & cour de Havre off rue St-Lazare. *Hours:* open 24 hours. *Métro:* St-Lazare (3, 12, 13). *Buses:* 20, 21, 22, 24, 26, 27, 28, 29, 32, 43, 49, 53, 66, 80, 81, 94, 95.

Église St-Augustin

Architecture buffs will want to see this church, built from 1860 to 1870 by Baltard, the famous architect of several large iron-and-glass canopied structures built for markets in Paris. Set amidst a busy, triangular intersection a few blocks west of the Gare St-Lazare, the church features twin towers, a large stained glass window above the entrance, and a dome with lots of iron trusses and framework inside. *Address:* place St-Augustin. *Métro:* St-Augustin (9). *Buses:* 22, 28, 32, 43, 49, 80, 84, 94.

Chapelle Expiatore

Commissioned by Louis XVIII and consecrated to the memory of Louis XVI and Marie-Antoinette, this two-story chapel is situated on the site of a cemetery where the bodies of the royal couple (until moved to St-Denis), Charlotte Corday (Marat's assassin), and 3,000 other victims of the Reign of Terror were buried in a mass grave. The relief above its entrance shows the King and Queen being transported to St-Denis, and their statues inside have displaced crowns at their feet. *Address:* Square Louis XVI (phone 42-65-35-80). *Hours:* summer: daily 10am-6pm; winter: 10am-4pm. *Métro:* St-Augustin (9), St-Lazare (3, 12, 13). *Buses:* 20, 21, 22, 32, 43, 49, 80, 94.

9th Arrondissement

The 9th arrondissement is perhaps the most interesting area in Paris. On its south end is the sumptuous Opéra and the main locations for the popular Au Printemps and Galeries Lafayette department stores. Going north, the area's character becomes more blue (-collar and otherwise) as you near Pigalle—a district famous for its strip shows, sex shops, and other forms of decadence. The 9th arrondissement also features the uninspired Grand Boulevards of Baron Haussmann and a few museums.

Its boundaries are boulevards Clichy and Rochechouart (north), boulevards de la Madeleine, des Capucines, des Italians, Montmartre, and Poissonnière (south), rue du Faubourg-Poissonnière (east), and rues Vignon, Tronchet, du Havre, and d'Amsterdam (west).

Opéra National de Paris-Garnier
Built 1860-75, the Opéra building is an exceptional example of the opulent Second Empire style. Its best features are an elaborate sweeping staircase, the gilded Grand Hall with statues, and the auditorium's five tiers of seats decorated in gold and red with a ceiling painted by Chagall. With the new Opéra at place de la Bastille (see 12th arrondissement), this building's entertainment is now limited primarily to dance and ballet. *Address:* place de l'Opera (phone 40-01-25-14). *Hours:* Mon-Sun 11am-5pm; closed Jan 1, May 1. *Métro:* Opéra (3, 7, 8). *Buses:* 20, 21, 22, 27, 29, 42, 52, 53, 66, 68, 81, 95. *Admission:* Ballet tickets start at 40F. Since a tour of the building costs about the same, you're better off attending a show and getting some entertainment for your francs.

Musée de la Parfumerie Fragonard
The history of perfume from ancient Egypt to the present is discussed through exhibits of bottles, perfume-burners, paintings,

and photographs. *Address:* 9 rue Scribe (phone 47-42-93-40). *Hours:* daily 9am-5:30pm; closed Dec 25 and Sundays from Oct 1-March 1. *Métro:* Opéra (3, 7, 8), Auber (A), Havre-Caumartin (3, 9). *Buses:* 20, 21, 42, 66, 81, 95.

Galeries Lafayette and Au Printemps

One of the best reasons to be in the 9th arrondissement is to visit the city's two premier department stores. Both have clothes, perfume, souvenirs, books, food, and about any item you could want, though most prices are no cheaper than back home. On a rainy day, the attractive stores (both consist of several buildings connected by skywalks) are great for browsing and people-watching. Au Printemp's rooftop café (9th floor) provides lunch-style food and excellent views of the Opéra quarter and north to Montmartre. Both stores also have free fashion shows weekly. (Tickets are in the free maps of Paris available at the entrances.) *Address:* Galeries Lafayette: 40 boulevard Haussmann (phone 42-82-36-40); Au Printemps: 64 boulevard Haussmann (phone 42-82-50-00). Both stores have smaller branches in other Paris locations. *Hours:* Mon-Sat 9:30am-7pm. *Métro:* Chausée d'Antin/La Fayette (7, 9), Havre Caumartin (3, 9), Auber (A). *Buses:* 20, 21, 22, 27, 42, 53, 68, 81, 95.

Église Trinité

Set on a pretty square a few blocks east of the Gare St-Lazare, this neo-Renaissance, Gothic Revival church (built 1863-67) boasts one of the tallest church towers in Paris. In front of its entrance, an interesting dual staircase leads to the square, accented by three fountains and marble sculpture. The church hosts free classical music concerts often. *Address:* place de la Trinité (off rue St-Lazare). *Métro:* Trinité (12). *Buses:* 26, 32, 43, 49, 68, 81, 89.

Musée Gustave Moreau

The museum dedicated to Gustave Moreau (1826-98), a leader of the Symbolist movement who also had a strong influence on modern artists like Matisse and Roualt, has an impressive display of 5,000 drawings, sketches, watercolors, and paintings— all housed in the prolific artist's former townhouse and studio. *Address:* 14 rue de la Rochefoucauld (phone 48-74-38-50). *Hours:* Mon & Wed 11am-5:15pm; Thur-Sun 10am-12:45pm & 2pm-5:15pm; closed Jan 1, May 1, Dec 25. *Métro:* Trinité (12).

Buses: 32, 81, 68, 28, 42. *Admission:* 13F on Sundays, 20F other days, Carte Musées et Monuments.

Musée de la Vie Romantique — Maison Scheffer

Housed in the 19th-century Italianate villa and twin studios of Dutch artist Ary Scheffer, this museum features the jewels and trinkets of author Georges Sand (no manuscripts) and Scheffer's art collection, which includes drawings by Ingres and Delacroix. Several exhibitions on 19th-century intellectuals, authors, and artists are held each year in the studios. *Address:* via a driveway at 16 rue Chaptal (phone 48-74-95-38). *Hours:* Tue-Sun 10am-5:50pm. *Métro:* Blanche (2), St-Georges (12). *Buses:* 72, 74, 67. *Admission:* 17.5F, Carte Musées et Monuments.

Fondation Dosne-Thiers

This small museum and affiliate of the Institut de France contains paintings and drawings about the Napoléonic Empire era. It's housed in an 1873 mansion on a picturesque, semi-circular place with a fountain and pretty garden. *Address:* 27 place St-Georges, off rue Notre-Dame de Lorette (phone 48-78-14-33). *Hours:* Thur-Fri noon-6pm; closed July 15-Aug 31. *Métro:* St-Georges (12). *Buses:* 67, 74. *Admission:* 17F

L'Astrolabe

Since I'm a travel writer, this is one of my favorite stores in Paris — a combined travel agency/travel bookstore with thousands of books and maps about every point on the globe. The maps, compared to their cost in the U.S. (due to import/export taxes), are extremely cheap. If you ever lose this book, remember that L'Astrolabe stocks it, plus my guide *France on the TGV* and a few other English-language titles. *Address:* 46 rue de Provence (also 14 rue Serpente in the 6th arrondissement). *Hours:* Mon-Sat 10am-7pm. *Métro:* Chausée d'Antin/La Fayette (7, 9), Le Peletier (7). *Buses:* 42, 68, 81.

À la Mère de Famille

This charming old shop has been selling chocolate, candy, jam, spices, condiments, wine, and other epicurean goodies from this location since 1761. Choose something that looks delicious (don't touch the merchandise — let the shopkeeper pick it up for you) and buy what you can afford; they'll sell even a quarter-kilo's worth. *Address:* 35 rue du Faubourg-Montmartre. *Hours:*

Mon-Sat 7:30am-1:30pm & 3pm-7pm. *Métro:* Le Peletier (7). *Buses:* 48, 67, 74, 85.

Musée du Grand Orient de France de la Franc-Maçonnerie Européene

In the rear of a Masonic Temple, this tiny museum displays Masonic insignia, paintings about the brotherhood, objects and robes used in ceremonies, and articles documenting the history of European Freemasonry. *Address:* 16 rue Cadet (phone 45-23-20-92). *Hours:* Mon-Sat 2pm-6pm. *Métro:* Cadet (7). *Buses:* 32, 42, 43, 48, 67, 74, 85.

Folies Bergère

This is the oldest (1869) and perhaps the most famous nightclub in Paris. If you're a dedicated reader of this book, you probably can't afford it, but the colorful posters advertising the current shows may be of interest. Plus, it's a Paris landmark. *Address:* 32 rue Richer. *Métro:* Cadet (7). *Buses:* 32, 43, 48, 85.

Hôtel Drouot

The Hôtel Drouot, the largest auction house in Paris, is a living museum, as thousands of objects are auctioned daily. If you see something you like (items range from extremely cheap to very expensive), be brave and make a bid. Appraisals in advance are free. It's even more interesting if you understand French, since there's always lively banter among participants. *Address:* 9 rue Drouot (phone 42-46-17-11). *Hours:* Mon-Sat 11am-6pm. *Métro:* Richelieu-Drouot (8, 9), Le Peletier (7). *Buses:* 67, 74, 85. *Admission:* free entry (10-18% commission to the house on purchased items).

Department de Musique Ancienne du Conservatoire Supérieur de Paris-CNR

Free classical, operatic, and other forms of instrumental and vocal music concerts are presented regularly by students from this music school. *Address:* Théatre Grévin at 10 boulevard Montmartre (phone 48-24-16-97). *Métro:* Rue Montmartre (8, 9). *Buses:* 20, 39, 48. 67, 74, 85.

10th Arrondissement

The 10th arrondissement is best known by travelers as the location of two large train stations, the Gare du Nord and Gare de l'Est. Although there are some good museums, monuments, and restaurants in the area—plus the picturesque Canal St-Martin—this commercial district is not a prime tourist area.

The boundaries of the 10th arrondissement are boulevard de la Chapelle (north), boulevards Bonne Nouvelle, St-Denis, and St-Martin, place de la République, and rue du Faubourg-du-Temple (south), boulevard de la Villette (east), and rue du Faubourg-Poissonnière (west).

Place de la République Monument

At the center of a large rectangular place, where the 3rd, 10th, and 11th arrondissements converge, a large monument (erected in 1880) honors France's return to Republican rule. One of the city's largest Métro stations is beneath the pavement. *Address:* Nine streets enter the place, including avenue de la République, rues du Temple and Faubourg-du-Temple, and boulevards du Temple and Voltaire. *Métro:* République (3, 5, 8, 9, 11). *Buses:* 20, 54, 56, 65, 75.

Canal St-Martin

The 19th-century Canal St-Martin was built as a shortcut from north Paris to the Seine River to avoid the long western loop the river takes as it snakes around the city. The 4.5-kilometer canal has nine locks and flows underground from square Frédérick-Lemaître to the Port de Plaisance de Paris-Arsenal at place de la Bastille. With quais lined with shops, cafés, 19th-century houses, small workshops, and service businesses, accented by arched bridges over the canal and pretty squares, it's a good locale to take a peaceful stroll and watch the barges. The most scenic section is between rue du Faubourg-du-Temple and square Eugène-Varlin. *Métro:* République (3, 5, 8, 9, 11), Goincourt (11), Château Landon (7). *Buses:* 46, 75.

Porte St-Denis
On the border of the 10th and 2nd arrondissements, just beyond the original entrance to the city walls during King Charles V's reign, is a 72-foot high triumphal arch. Built in 1672 to resemble the Arch of Titus in Rome, it is dedicated to King Louis XIV's military victories in Holland. *Address:* boulevard St-Denis *Métro:* Strasbourg-St-Denis (4, 8, 9). *Buses:* 20, 38, 39, 47.

Porte St-Martin
On the border of the 10th and 3rd arrondissements, a smaller triumphal arch (56-feet high) was built in 1674 to honor King Louis XIV's military victories over the Dutch, Spanish, and German armies. *Address:* boulevard St-Martin. *Métro:* Strasbourg-St-Denis (4, 8, 9). *Buses:* 20, 38, 39, 47.

Marché Château-d'Eau
For a good look at Old World Paris, visit this covered food market, where you'll see butchers carving slabs of meat and washing them in the market's fountain, and grandmothers shopping with small carts and wicker baskets. *Address:* rue du Château-d'Eau at rue Bouchardon. *Hours:* Tue-Sun 8am-7:30pm. *Métro:* Château-d'Eau (4). *Buses:* 38, 39, 47, 54, 56, 65.

Office du Tourisme: Bureau Gare du Nord
This branch of the Office du Tourisme, where you can get free maps and literature about Paris, is set in one of the best examples of a 19th-century train station (though its interior has been severely modernized for the TGV Nord line). Built in 1863 by German architect Jacob Ignaz Hittorf, the Gare du Nord's best features are its 600-foot-long, neoclassical façade with statues of military greats along the main window, Roman figures at its roof line, and the steel and glass vaulting over the train platforms. Trains depart this station to northern France, Belgium, Holland, northern Germany, Scandinavia, and England via the English Channel Tunnel. *Address:* rue de Dunkerque at place Napoléon III (phone 45-26-94-82). *Hours:* May 1-Oct 31: Mon-

Sat 8am-9pm; Nov 1-April 30: Mon-Sat, 8am-8pm. *Métro:* Gare du Nord (4, 5, B, D). *Buses:* 42, 43, 46, 47, 48, 49, 350.

Église St-Vincent-de-Paul

Resembling a Greek temple with narrow Gothic towers, the Église St-Vincent-de-Paul, commissioned by King Louis Philippe in 1844, is another Hittdorf creation. On its triangular front pediment, a bas-relief features religious allegories about the work of its namesake, the Apostle of Charity, who dedicated his life to caring for the sick, disabled, and homeless. At the top of its entrance are statues of apostles and other evangelists. Inside, take a look at the decorated pulpit and the Lady Chapel, which offers eight scenes from the life of the Virgin. *Address:* place Franz Liszt. *Métro:* Poissonnière (7). *Buses:* 32, 42, 48, 49.

Musée Baccarat

Over 1,200 items of crystal bearing the Baccarat name detail the evolution of crystalware from 1828 to the present. Objects range from mirror glass to abstract sculptures. The museum also presents an interesting video showing how the pieces are made. *Address:* 30 bis rue de Paradis. *Hours:* Mon-Fri 9am-6pm, Sat 10am-noon & 2pm-5pm. *Métro:* Gare de l'Est (4, 5, 7), Poissonnière (7). *Buses:* 32. *Admission:* 10F.

Galerie Le Monde d'Art

This former headquarters of the Boulanger China Company is now a gallery showing interesting exhibits of ceramic tiles. It also hosts temporary exhibitions by modern dissident artists. *Address:* 10 rue Paradis. *Hours:* Mon 2pm-7pm, Tue-Sat 1pm-7pm. *Métro/Buses:* same as Musée Baccarat.

Office du Tourisme: Bureau Gare de l'Est

Only a few blocks east of the Gare du Nord, there's another 19th-century train station and a branch of the Office du Tourisme, where you can get free maps and literature about Paris. Trains depart this station for northeast/east France and central/south Germany. It's also the future home of the TGV Est, slated to travel to Reims, Nancy, Strasbourg, and Germany. *Address:* place du 11 Novembre 1918 (phone 46-07-17-73). *Hours:* May 1-Oct 31: Mon-Sat 8am-9pm; Nov 1-April 30: Mon-Sat 8am-8pm. *Métro:* Gare de l'Est (4, 5, 7). *Buses:* 30, 31, 32, 38, 39, 350.

Église St-Laurent

One of oldest churches in Paris is just a few blocks south of the Gare de l'Est. It's had numerous alterations since its foundation was laid in the 15th century, so it's a real hodgepodge of architectural styles. Take a look at the neo-Gothic façade added in 1860, a bas-relief carving of God in the north portal, and the 15th-century choir (later decorated in a 17th-century Baroque style). *Address:* 68 boulevard Magenta at boulevard de Strasbourg. *Métro:* Gare de l'Est (4, 5, 7). *Buses:* 38, 39, 46, 47, 54, 56, 65.

Marché St-Quentin

Beneath this large, iron-and-glass canopied building (circa 1866), a huge food market sells everything from rabbits to truffles. The vast scale of this operation is reminiscent of the former Les Halles market. In the center of the market stands an original Wallace fountain. (Approximately 100 of these short, green fountains were placed in Paris squares and parks in the late 1800's to provide free drinking water. The metal cups attached to them were removed in the 1950's due to stricter sanitation laws.) There are rumors that this market will be torn down soon, so see it while you can. *Address:* 85 boulevard Magenta. *Hours:* Tue-Sat 8am-1pm & 3:30pm-7:30pm; Sun 8am-1pm. *Métro/ Buses:* same as Église St-Laurent.

11th Arrondissement

The 11th arrondissement, traditionally a blue-collar district and home to many of the city's immigrants, today is gaining a new look as artists, restauranteurs, and other young professionals move into the area from the increasingly expensive Left Bank. Though it's not much of a tourist area, it can be interesting to walk its streets, see how another part of Paris lives, and check out the new galleries and restaurants.

The 11th arrondissement's boundaries are rue du Faubourg-du-Temple (north), rue du Faubourg-St-Antoine (south), boulevards de Belleville, de Charonne, and de Ménilmontant (east), and boulevards Voltaire, Richard Lenoir, and place de la Bastille (west).

Tati
This is another location for the terrific discount department chain. (See the main listing in the 6th arrondissement.) *Address:* 13 place de la République. *Métro:* République (3, 5, 8, 9, 11). *Buses:* 20, 54, 56, 65, 75.

Cirque d'Hiver
On the border of the 3rd and 11th arrondissements, this unique building with 20 sides was built specifically for the circus in 1852. The circus still performs here today (150F per person). *Address:* 110 rue Amelot. *Métro:* Filles du Calvaire (8). *Buses:* 65, 96.

Musée Édith Piaf
This small, private museum displays belongings, letters, photographs, records, and other items relating to the career of the famed *chansonnier* Edith Piaf. *Address:* 5 rue Crespin du Gast (phone 43-55-52-72). *Hours:* Mon-Thur 1pm-6pm, by appointment only. *Métro:* Ménilmontant (2). *Buses:* 96.

Église Ste-Marguerite

If you walk past this rather plain church, you'll miss one of the prettiest church interiors in Paris. Built in 1624 to accommodate the growing suburb of artisans who lived and worked in the area, its sanctuary features several bas-reliefs of Biblical scenes, paintings from the 16th-18th centuries, a chapel dedicated to the souls of Purgatory, and *trompe-l'oeil* wall paintings by Brunetti. Its garden is dedicated to Raoul Nordling, the Swedish consul who dissuaded the Nazis from blowing up Paris in 1944. The cemetery supposedly holds the body of Louis XVII, the ten-year-old heir to the throne who was rumored to have died in the Temple prison (see 3rd arrondissement). *Address:* 36 rue St-Bernard. *Métro:* Ledruc-Rollin (8). *Buses:* 46, 76, 86.

Emmaüs

The charitable Emmaüs organization operates a group of thrift stores in the Paris area (this is the only location within the city limits) with lots of clothes, household goods, and books. If you don't mind the crowds and some digging, you might find a bargain-priced "Made in France" item. *Address:* 54 rue de Charonne. *Hours:* Mon-Wed & Fri 2pm-5:30pm, Thur & Sat 9:30am-5:30pm. *Métro:* Ledruc-Rollin (8). *Buses:* 76, 86.

Rue de Lappe

Although long past their 1930's heyday, a few *bal musettes* (music halls) remain on this street that were frequented by Edith Piaf, Rita Hayworth, and other stars. Several new art galleries have also opened on this street and the nearby rues de Charonne and Keller. *Métro:* Bastille (1, 5, 8). *Buses:* 69, 76.

Rue du Faubourg-St-Antoine

The rue du Faubourg-St-Antoine passes through a district known for its craftsmen, whose principal trade was furniture-making. Some of the workshops, most family-run for generations, still operate in the interconnecting courtyards and narrow, open-air passages (also identified by *cour* or *cité*) that divide buildings and provide shortcuts to other streets. Most of the craftsman will gladly answer your questions about their creations and take your orders. *Address:* primarily between avenue Ledruc-Rollin and place de la Bastille. *Métro:* Bastille (1, 5, 8), Ledruc-Rollin (8). *Buses:* 76.

FNAC Music Shop

The FNAC store at this location focuses on music. In a special section of the store, you can listen to CDs all day if you like, as long as people aren't waiting behind you. When you see the area where people have headphones on, look for an empty slot and make your choices by touching a computer screen (*touchez l'ecran*). *Address:* 4 place de la Bastille. *Hours:* Mon-Tue, Thur, Sat 10am-8pm; Wed & Fri 10am-10pm. *Métro/Buses:* same as Opéra de Paris-Bastille.

Square de la Roquette

After touring the Père Lachaise cemetery in the nearby 20th arrondissement, cross the boulevard de Ménilmontant via rue de la Roquette for two blocks and relax in the 11th arrondissement's largest park. Built on the site of a former prison, the hilly park features a variety of trees and flowers, two *boules* courts, and several play areas for children. *Address:* enter from rues de la Roquette, Servan, or Merlin. *Métro:* Père Lachaise (2, 3), Philippe Auguste (2). *Buses:* 61, 69.

Jardin de la Cité-Beauharnis

The best feature of this modern park, also near Père Lachaise, is a gigantic sundial made from concrete and stainless steel, which casts its shadow on a semi-circular court. Scattered throughout the park are more concrete creations, some resembling dinosaurs and letters. *Address:* enter from rue Léon Frot via cité Beauharnis or rue des Neuve Boulets. *Métro:* Charonne (9), Boulets-Montreuil (9). *Buses:* 56, 76.

12th Arrondissement

The 12th arrondissement, anchored on the west by the Opéra building at place de la Bastille and on the east by the Bois de Vincennes, is basically an extension of the 11th arrondissement's blue-collar district. Though the area near the Opéra is going upscale, this is still working-class Paris—although slightly more interesting than the 11th, thanks to revitalization programs that are creating new parks and modern buildings.

The boundaries of the 12th arrondissement are rue du Faubourg-St-Antoine and cours de Vincennes (north), Seine River (south), Bois de Vincennes and boulevard Périphérique (east), and place de la Bastille and boulevard de la Bastille (west).

Opéra National de Paris-Bastille

At the southeast corner of busy place de la Bastille, the Opéra de Paris-Bastille features a gleaming, curved-glass façade and a mass of jumbled shapes. Criticized by taxpayers for its cost (2.1 billion francs) and by residents for "ruining" their neighborhood, the Opéra opened with great fanfare during the 1989 bicentennial celebration of the French Revolution. It's a must-see for architecture buffs. *Address:* 120 rue de Lyon at place de la Bastille (phone 40-01-19-70). *Métro:* Bastille (1, 5, 8). *Buses:* 20, 29, 65, 69, 76, 86, 87, 91. *Admission:* tickets start at 50F.

Jardin de l'Arsenal

The narrow, terraced Jardin de l'Arsenal, with a rose garden and pergolas, offers pleasant views of the Port de Plaisance de Paris-Arsenal, a marina for 200 pleasure craft with access to the Seine River and Canal St-Martin. The basin is the former moat skirting the ramparts of King Charles V's palace. *Address:* east side of the Port, off boulevard de la Bastille. *Métro:* Bastille (1, 5, 8), quai de la Rapée (5). *Buses:* 20, 24, 29, 57, 63, 65, 87, 91.

Promenade Plantée/Viaduc des Arts

This former bed of an elevated railway line (in service from 1859-1969), which runs along avenue Daumesnil from the rear of the Opéra de Paris-Bastille to the Bois de Vincennes, has become a park and promenade—a 4.5-mile path lined with flowers, benches, and sidewalks. At street level, beneath the 30-foot high vaulted viaduct, are retail shops, artisans' workshops, restaurants, and other businesses. *Address:* follows avenue Daumesnil to the Jardin de Reuilly. From there, the promenade follows the rail line northwest to square Charles-Péguy, then returns south to rejoin avenue Daumesnil near Porte Dorée. *Métro:* Bastille (1, 5, 8), Gare de Lyon (1, A), Daumesnil (6, 8), Michel Bizot (8), Porte Dorée (8). *Buses:* 29, 46.

V.I.A. (Valorisation de l'Innovation dans l'Ameublement)

Founded by the Ministry of Industry, this organization assists interior designers and promotes new furniture. Its showrooms are open to the public. *Address:* 29-37 avenue Daumesnil. *Hours:* Mon & Sat 11am-7pm, Tue-Fri 10:30am-7pm. *Métro:* Châtelet (1, 4, 7, 11). *Buses:* 21, 67, 69, 70, 72, 76, 81, 85.

Place d'Aligre Market

An interesting assortment of second-hand clothes, books, prints, bric-à-brac, buttons, and other junk is sold at this small flea market, some at extremely cheap prices. You can also buy your lunch here from the adjoining stalls selling fruit, cheese, and vegetables. *Address:* access off rue du Faubourg-St-Antoine via rue d'Aligre. *Hours:* Tue-Sun 8am-1pm. *Métro:* Ledruc-Rollin (8). *Buses:* 61, 86.

Office du Tourisme: Bureau Gare de Lyon

This is another convenient branch of the Office du Tourisme, where you can get free maps and literature about Paris. This station is home to the TGV Sud-Est (the first train to provide high-speed rail service in Europe) and other trains departing for east/southeast France, Switzerland, and Italy. It's also the location of **Le Train Bleu**, a historic Belle Epoque restaurant. *Address:* cour Diderot (phone 43-43-33-24). *Hours:* May 1-Oct 31: Mon-Sat 8am-9pm; Nov 1-April 30: Mon-Sat 8am-8pm. *Métro:* Gare de Lyon (1, A). *Buses:* 20, 57, 61, 63, 65, 87, 91.

Ministrie de l'Économie des Finances & Palais Omnisports

The odd, modern building with a slender finger jutting over quai de Bercy into the Seine River houses the offices of the Ministry of Economy and Finance. Across the street, thrust into a manmade hill, is the bunker-looking Palais Omnisports, where 17,000 people can watch sports (from ice hockey to auto racing), concerts, and other events. Both of these buildings mark the first phase of a massive revitalization program (see below) for the former village of Bercy, whose wine warehouse district had fallen into disrepair. *Address:* between Seine River and rue de Bercy. *Hours:* Ministrie de l'Économie closed to the public; hours vary for Palais Omnisports, depending on event. *Métro:* Quai de la Gare (6), Bercy (6) *Buses:* 24, 87. *Admission:* cheap seats available for some events at Palais Omnisports.

Parc de Bercy and Bercy Redevelopment Zone

When completed, this slender park will provide a green, flower-lined path along the Seine River from the Palais Omnisports to a point past the Pont de Tolbiac. Surrounding it will be new hotels, restaurants, the Centre Culturel Americain (see below), Bercy Expo (business center for international foods), Cité Viti-Vinicole (trading facilities for Bercy wholesale wine merchants), a conference center, a 17-screen cinema, and numerous shops. *Address/Métro/Buses:* same as Palais Omnisports.

Église St-Esprit

Although most churches built in the 20th century in Paris are uninspiring, this one's worth seeing. Made from concrete in 1931, it features a 275-foot tower, interesting mosaics and frescos, and a wall painting in the upper gallery depicting world evangelism by celebrated missionaries. *Address:* 186 avenue Daumesnil. *Métro:* Daumesnil (6, 8). *Buses:* 29, 46, 62.

Place de la Nation

Place de la Nation is the second-largest traffic circle in Paris (after place Charles-de-Gaulle at the Arc de Triomphe), with cars entering its hub from 11 directions. On the east side, two columns and pavilions mark the site of a Paris toll house and the ceremonial entry point for the Kings of France since the 17th century. Opposite this entrance, there are several good retail stores, including a branch of Au Printemps and Inno (see *Miscellaneous Paris Bargains*). *Address:* major streets entering the place include rue du Faubourg-St-Antoine, avenue Philippe Auguste, cours de Vincennes, and boulevards Diderot and Voltaire. *Métro:* Nation (1, 2, 6, 9, A). *Buses:* 56, 86, 351.

Bois de Vincennes

The city's largest park (2,458 acres) contains a myriad of sights including the Château de Vincennes, Musée des Arts Africains et Océaniens, Parc Floral, Hippodrome de Vincennes (all below), Buddhist Center, Catoucherie de Vincennes (four theater companies housed in an old ammunitions factory), and the largest zoo in France, with over 600 mammals and 200 species of birds. The park has numerous hiking trails and hosts festivals throughout the year. *Address:* southeast corner of Paris via avenue Daumesnil. *Hours:* park open 24 hours; see below for times of specific sights. *Métro:* Porte Dorée (8), Château de Vincennes (1). *Buses:* 24, 46, 56, 86, 87, PC. *Admission:* free for park (specific sights may charge a fee).

Château de Vincennes

Although it's called a château, this is a medieval fortress, complete with ten-foot-thick walls, a moat, a large keep, and a dungeon. Built in the 14th century to surround a 12th-century royal hunting lodge, the château has been used as a royal residence, prison, arsenal, and army barracks. *Address:* avenue de Paris, on north edge of Bois de Vincennes (phone 43-28-15-48). *Hours:* Oct 1-March 10: Wed-Mon 11:30am-4pm; April 1-Sep 30: Wed-Mon 9:30-noon & 1:30pm-5pm. *Métro:* Château de Vincennes (1). *Buses:* 46, 56. *Admission:* Carte Musées et Monuments.

Parc Floral

The Parc Floral is the prettiest section of the Bois de Vincennes, with the best variety of flowers and shrubs in Paris. Created in 1969, its 70 acres feature a combination of colorful, artistically arranged flower gardens, lily ponds that Monet would want to paint if he were alive, a vegetable garden, and sculpture by international artists. Visit in the spring and early summer when everything is blooming. Large flower exhibitions are held here every season. *Address:* a few steps south of the Château de

Vincennes. *Hours:* daily 9:30am-8pm. *Métro/Buses:* same as Château de Vincennes. *Admission:* 5F.

Hippodrome de Vincennes

This horse-racing track (trotters), on the southeast corner of the Bois de Vincennes, is one of three inside the Paris city limits. Inexpensive seats are always available, except during annual races, when all seats are sold months in advance. *Address:* avenue Gravelle (phone 43-68-35-39). *Hours:* check newspaper sports page for race times. *Métro:* Joinville-le-Pont (A-2). *Buses:* 24, 87. *Admission:* 25F for cheapest seats.

Musée des Arts d'Afrique et d'Océanie

Built in 1931 for the Colonial Exhibition, this museum specializes in art from Oceania and Africa. An interesting sight in the basement is a pond with baby crocodiles, and there's an outstanding aquarium. *Address:* 293 avenue Daumesnil, on west edge of Bois de Vincennes (phone 43-43-14-54). *Hours:* Mon & Wed-Fri 10am-noon & 1:30-5:30pm; Sat & Sun 12:30pm-6pm. Closed May 1. *Métro:* Porte Dorée (8). *Buses:* 46, 87, PC. *Admission:* Carte Musées et Monuments.

/3th Arrondissement

The large, crescent-shaped 13th arrondissement is blue-collar Paris on the Left Bank, a combination of native Parisians and immigrants (including a large Asian contingency). If you want to see other cultures at work, take a stroll through this area during the day and visit the Asian markets, which will transport you to the Far East. The 13th's current major sight is the large Gobelins tapestry studio, where some of France's most famous tapestries have been manufactured, and in the future, the new Bibliothèque de France.

The boundaries of the 13th arrondissement are boulevards de Port Royal, St-Marcel, l'Hôpital, and Gare d'Austerlitz (north), boulevard Périphérique (south), Seine River (east), and rues de la Sainte and de l'Amiral Mouchez (west).

Office du Tourisme: Bureau Gare d'Austerlitz

Within the large Gare d'Austerlitz (note the Métro train passing through its upper level), a branch of the Office du Tourisme distributes free maps and literature about Paris. Trains originating here travel to Brittany and the Loire Valley, central and southwest France, and Spain. The TGV Atlantique, which travels to many of the same locations from the Gare Montparnasse, has limited service from this location. *Address:* place Valhubert (phone 47-26-94-82). *Hours:* May 1-Oct 31: Mon-Sat 8am-9pm; Nov 1-April 30: Mon-Sat 8am-3pm. *Métro:* Gare d'Austerlitz (5, 10, C). *Buses:* 24, 57, 63, 61, 65, 89, 91.

Hôpital de la Salpêtrière and Chapelle St-Louis

The mammoth building next to the Gare d'Austerlitz is a large psychiatric hospital built during King Louis XIV's reign to house homeless people. It's also where Freud witnessed Jean Charcot's experiments on hysteria. The building's lantern-topped, octagonal-domed Chapelle St-Louis (built in 1670) contains eight naves so the sick could be separated from the insane and poor. Free organ concerts are held here, and the building has surprisingly good acoustics. *Address:* square Marie-Curie, off boulevard de l'Hôpital. *Métro:* Gare d'Austerlitz (5, 10, C), St-Marcel (5). *Buses:* 57, 91. *Admission:* free to enter library and chapel.

Bibliothèque Nationale de France-Mitterrand

The city's newest library, another controversial architectural project, was built on an old freight yard across the Seine River from the Palais Omnisports and Parc Bercy. The ultra-modern facility features four glass-and-steel towers at the corners of a large open square with a sunken garden. It is the new depository for the books from the Bibliothèque Nationale. *Address:* 11 quai François Mauriac, 9 boulevard Vincent Auriol (phone 44-23-03-70). *Métro:* quai de la Gare (6). *Buses:* 62. *Admission:* parts of the facility will be free without a library card.

Quai de la Gare Artists

The old refrigerator warehouses, located south of the Gare d'Austerlitz between the railroad tracks and Seine River, are being renovated by artists for use as studios and living quarters. At random times during the year, several artists arrange group shows and offer studio tours. *Address:* quai de la Gare, between Pont de Tolbiac and Pont National. *Métro:* Boulevard Masséna (C). *Buses:* 62, PC.

Quartier Géneral de l'Armée de Salut Thrift Store

The Paris Salvation Army is headquartered in a unique 1932 Le Corbusier building—one of the first in Paris with sealed windows and air-conditioning. If you're down-and-out, they'll supply you with free clothes, food, and lodging. (A floating hotel for the truly homeless is on a barge in the Seine River near the Gare d'Austerlitz.) The organization also operates a thrift store selling clothes, furniture, household items, books, etc. at extremely cheap prices. Everyday, 16 trucks unload items collected from the attics and cellars of Parisians. Get there early for the best stuff—though you'll have to compete with professional dealers searching for antiques and other overlooked valuables. *Address:* 12 rue Cantagrel (phone 45-83-54-50). *Hours:* Thrift Store: Tue-Sat 9am-noon & 2pm-6pm. *Métro:* Boulevard Masséna (C). *Buses:* PC.

La Cité Fleurie

Behind the walls of an old prison amid an overgrown garden, you'll find 27 artist's studios—the addresses in past years of Rodin, Picasso, Gauguin, and Modigliani. Upon request, some artists will invite you inside to see their latest works. *Address:* 65 boulevard Arago. *Hours:* varies by studio. *Métro:* St-Jacques (6). *Buses:* 21, Orlybus.

Guignol du Parc Choisy

The puppetry company in Parc Choisy has been entertaining children and adults for decades with its slapstick humor. Even though the show's in French, it's a quaint theatrical art form worth seeing. *Address:* 149 avenue de Choisy (phone 43-66-72-39). *Hours:* Wed, Sat, & holidays 3:30pm. *Métro:* Place d'Italie (5, 6, 7). *Buses:* 27, 47, 57, 67, 83. *Admission:* 12F for puppet show.

Chinatown

A large Chinese and Asian population lives south of Parc Choisy. For unusual sights, sounds, and smells, take a walk through Chinatown during the day. *Address:* approximate boundaries are rue de Tolbiac (north), avenue d'Ivry (east), avenue d'Italie (west), & boulevard Masséna (south). *Métro:* Tolbiac (7), Maison Blanche (7), Port d'Italie (7). *Buses:* 47, 62.

14th Arrondissement

To the arts and culture crowd, the 14th arrondissement is only Montparnasse (north part of the arrondissement), whose cafés were made famous by Hemingway, Fitzgerald, and their ilk during the 1920's and 30's. Although the cafés no longer attract such famous clientele, they are still watering holes for those who want to be seen. The rest of the primarily blue-collar arrondissement boasts a few good museums, an observatory, and the pretty Parc Montsouris at the southeast corner.

The 14th arrondissement's boundaries are boulevards Montparnasse and de Port Royal (north), boulevard Périphérique (south), rues de la Sainte and de l'Amiral Mouchez (east), and rue Vercingétorix, place de la Catalogne, and Gare Montparnasse (west).

Lion de Belfort Monument
In the middle of the busy traffic intersection place Denfert-Rochereau, this lion sculpture on a pedestal is actually a smaller copy of Frédéric-Auguste Bartholdi's (creator of the Statue of Liberty) memorial to Colonel Denfert-Rochereau, who defended Belfort in 1871 against the Prussian army during the Franco-Prussian War. *Address:* place Denfert-Rochereau. *Métro:* Denfert-Rochereau (4, 6, B). *Buses:* 38, 68, Orlybus.

Barrière d'Enfer
The two customs houses built here in 1784 were christened the "hell barrier" due to the exorbitant tolls extorted on all who passed through its gates. One of the houses is now used as the entrance to the Catacombes (see below). Of the 42 customs houses built at Paris's outer walls, these are two of only four left; the rest were destroyed during the French Revolution because they represented the Ancien Regime. *Address/Métro/Buses:* same as Lion de Belfort monument.

Catacombes
With its nearly endless maze of tunnels, the underground depository for the bones of six million dead from the ancient cemeteries of Paris was used as a hiding place by the French Resistance during World War II. Although the famous are supposedly buried in other Parisian cemeteries, their remains may be here instead. If you tour this macabre sight, take a flashlight, wear a coat, and stay close to your guide, since people have gotten lost—and never found. *Address:* 1 place Denfert-Rochereau (phone 43-22-47-63). *Hours:* Tue-Fri 2pm-4pm; Sat & Sun 9am-11am & 2pm-4pm. *Métro/Buses:* same as Lion de Belfort monument. *Admission:* Carte Musées et Monuments.

Observatoire de Paris &
Musée de l'Observatoire de Paris
The Observatoire de Paris was the world's first modern observatory (circa 1667). Each side of the building aligns exactly with the north, south, east, and west headings of a compass. (The south side determines the official Paris latitude of 48° 50'11"N.) In addition to the building, which was constructed from stone instead of wood (risk of fire) or iron (the magnetic effect), there are a nice park and fountain on the grounds. The museum (too expensive for this book's guidelines) displays instruments related to astronomy. *Address:* 61 avenue de l'Observatoire (phone 40-51-22-21). *Hours:* May 1-July 31: daily 9am-5pm. *Métro:* St-Jacques (6), Port-Royal (B). *Buses:* 38, 68, 83, 91. *Admission:* park and exterior views of the building are free.

Cimetière de Montparnasse
Several famous French are interred in this 44-acre cemetery, including author, philosopher, and Existentialist leader Jean-Paul Sartre and his lover Simone de Beauvoir (they share a grave), poet Baudelaire, author Maupassant, playwright Beckett, sculptors Bourdelle, Zadkine, Laurens, Bartholdi, and Brancusi, composer Saint-Saëns, and industrialist André Citroën. To find these and other celebrity tombs, obtain the free *Index des Celebrités* at the main entrance. *Address:* enter off boulevard Edgar Quintet (main entrance) or rue Froidevaux. *Métro:* Edgar Quintet (6), Raspail (4, 6), Denfert-Rochereau (4, 6, B), Gaîté (13). *Buses:* 28, 58, 68, 82, 91.

Place de Catalogne and Les Colonnes

Created by Spanish architect Ricardo Bofill, the circular place de Catalogne behind the Gare Montparnasse features a massive tilted stone disk at its center, from which water cascades down to form a fountain. On a corner of the traffic circle, a square arch with two large, unadorned Doric columns beckons you into the circular Les Colonnes, an office/apartment complex bounded by glass walls and a colonnade of four-sided glass columns with stone capitals. *Address:* intersected by rue Vercingétorix. *Métro:* Montparnasse-Bienvenüe (4, 6, 12, 13), Gaîté (13). *Buses:* 28, 58.

Gaîté-Montparnasse

For late-night recreation, this complex features 16 bowling lanes, pool tables, video games, a bar, and a *brasserie*. Even if you don't participate, there's always a fun crowd to hang out with. *Address:* 25 rue du Commandant René-Mouchotte, across from Gare Montparnasse. *Hours:* Mon-Thur & Sun 10am-2am; Fri-Sat 10am-4am. *Métro:* Montparnasse-Bienvenüe (4, 6, 12, 13). *Buses:* 28, 48, 58, 82, 89, 91, 92, 94, 95, 96. *Admission:* 20F for bowling, less for pool and video games.

Utopia

For good blues music and relatively cheap drinks (50F), check out this club popular with area students. *Address:* 1 rue Nièpce. *Hours:* Tue-Sat 8:30pm-dawn. *Métro:* Pernety (13). *Buses:* 58.

Parc Montsouris

Doubling as an arboretum, the large Parc Montsouris, built in 1868 by Baron Haussmann, features hundreds of species of trees (all labeled) and a contingent of ducks, geese, and swans who enjoy the artificial lake. Although it's intersected by RER line B (in an open channel), it's one of the prettier Paris parks, with some interesting sculpture by Arp, Bourdelle, Brancusi, and others decorating the lawn around the lake. Free concerts are held at the bandstand in the summer. *Address:* enter off avenue Reille (north), boulevard Jourdan (south), rue Gazan (east), or rue Nansouty (west). *Métro:* Cité Universitaire (B). *Buses:* 21, Orlybus.

Marionettes de Montsouris
There are marionette performances three days a week in Parc Montsouris. *Address:* northwest corner of park. *Hours:* one-hour shows Wed & Sun at 2:30pm, 3:30pm, & 4:30pm; Sat 2:30pm & 3:30pm. *Métro/Buses:* same as Parc Montsouris. *Admission:* 15F.

Cité Universitaire
If you want to meet people from over 122 countries, pop into one of the 44 dormitories that make up this vast complex located across the street from the Parc Montsouris. Students are usually a good source for the latest inexpensive happenings in the city. *Address:* between boulevards Jourdan and Périphérique. *Métro:* Cité Universitaire (B). *Buses:* 21, 67, Orlybus.

Villa Seurat
A few blocks northwest of Parc Montsouris is a narrow, dead-end street where the famous artists and writers Dali, Seurat, Soutine, Anaïs Nin, Henry Miller, and Lawrence Durrell had residences. *Address:* off rue de la Tombe-Issoire. *Métro:* Alésia (4). *Buses:* 62.

Musée Lenine
Lenin's apartment, where he lived with his wife Kroupskaia and her mother from 1909 to 1912, is now a small museum with exhibits concerning his three years in Paris. *Address:* 4 rue Marie-Rose (phone 42-79-99-58). *Hours:* Mon-Fri 9:30am-5pm, by appointment only; closed July. *Métro:* Alésia (4). *Buses:* 62, PC.

Marché aux Puces de la Porte de Vanves
On the south edge of Paris, this large flea market has the best selection of extremely cheap items in town. *Address:* avenue Georges Lafenestre (some unlicensed dealers on avenue Marc Sangnier). *Hours:* Sat & Sun 7am-7:30pm. *Métro:* Porte de Vanves (13). *Buses:* 42, 58, 95, PC.

15th Arrondissement

It's not a total tourist backwater, but the 15th arrondissement is primarily residential, home to both blue-collar and middle-class families. By walking its streets at random, you'll discover the shops, markets, and parks used by the average Parisian. Its major monument is the modern Tour Montparnasse, a 56-story Paris landmark. Beneath it, the Gare Montparnasse is one of the biggest train stations in Europe. As the largest arrondissement in Paris, the 15th also has some interesting museums and inexpensive restaurants favored by the locals.

The boundaries of the 15th arrondissement are avenues de Suffren and de Saxe, rue de Sèvres, and boulevard Montparnasse (north), boulevard Périphérique (south), rues Julia Barret and Vercingétorix, place de la Catalogne, and Gare Montparnasse (east), and Seine River (west).

Office du Tourisme: Bureau Gare Montparnasse

This branch of the Office du Tourisme, where you can get free maps and literature about Paris, is located in the modern, five-level Gare Montparnasse, the largest train station in Paris. While you're here, take a look at the sleek, silver TGV Atlantique trains, which travel up to 187mph en route to destinations in Brittany, the Loire Valley, southwest France, and Spain. *Address:* 15 boulevard de Vaugirard (phone 43-22-19-19). *Hours:* May 1-Oct 31: Mon-Sat 8am-9pm; Nov 1-April 30: Mon-Sat 8am-8pm. *Métro:* Montparnasse-Bienvenüe (4, 6, 12, 13). *Buses:* 28, 48, 58, 82, 89, 91, 92, 94, 95, 96, Air France.

Jardin Atlantique

This unique park in Paris is above the railroad tracks as an upper-level extension of the Gare Montparnasse. It features a central fountain, large grassy areas, rose gardens, and five tennis courts. *Address:* enter through the Gare Montparnasse or off the Pont des Cinqs-Martyrs-du-Lycée-Buffon. *Métro/Buses:* same as Gare Montparnasse.

Memorial du Maréchal Leclerc de Hauteclocque et de la Libération de Paris et Musée Jean Moulin

Paris's newest museum honors the valiant efforts of two of France's most recognized WWII heroes. Utilizing modern technology and vivid audio-video displays, the museum allows visitors to follow in Moulin's footsteps and then see how Leclerc led the Free French Army to liberate Paris in 1944. *Address:* same as Jardin Atlantique (phone 40-64-39-44). *Hours:* Tue-Sun 10am-5:40pm. *Métro/Buses:* same as Gare Montparnasse. *Admission:* 18F.

Musée de la Poste

The postal history museum across the street from the Gare Montparnasse displays French and international stamps from 1849 to the present, postal uniforms, sorting machines, and a balloon used to send mail during the 1870 Prussian siege of Paris. *Address:* 34 boulevard de Vaugirard (phone 42-79-24-24). *Hours:* Mon-Sat 10am-6pm. *Métro:* Montparnasse-Bienvenüe (4, 6, 12, 13). *Buses:* 28, 48, 91, 92, 94, 95, 96. *Admission:* Carte Musées et Monuments.

Musée Antoine Bourdelle

The studio and home of sculptor Antoine Bourdelle, where he lived from 1884 until his death in 1929, is now a museum and major showcase for his work. Bourdelle was heavily influenced by Rodin, and the museum's sculpture, plaster casts, portrait busts, and drawings depict his attempts to bridge 19th-century art and the modern age. *Address:* 16/18 rue Antoine Bourdelle (phone 45-48-67-27). *Hours:* Tue-Sun 10am-5:40pm. *Métro:* Montparnasse-Bienvenüe (4, 6, 12, 13). *Buses:* 28, 82, 89, 91, 92, 94, 95, 96. *Admission:* Carte Musées et Monuments.

Musée de l'Institut Pasteur

This small museum, located within the research institute Louis Pasteur founded in 1887, includes exhibits illustrating the scientist's medical experiments (pasteurization, treatment for rabies, etc.), his laboratory and apartment with furnishings, and a crypt holding his body. Still a working research facility, the Pasteur Institute was responsible for isolating the AIDS virus in 1983. *Address:* 25 rue du Dr. Roux (phone 45-68-82-82). *Hours:* Mon-Fri 2pm-5:30pm. *Métro:* Pasteur (6, 12), Volontaires (12). *Buses:* 39, 48, 70. *Admission:* 15F.

Ambassade d'Australie

In the lobby of the Australian embassy, a large exhibition space houses temporary art exhibitions. The embassy also sponsors a number of other activities and keeps a library available to the public. *Address:* 4 rue Jean-Rey (phone 45-75-62-00). *Hours:* depends on event. *Métro:* Champ de Mars/Tour Eiffel (C), Bir-Hakeim (6, C). *Buses:* 82.

Village Suisse

Opposite the École Militaire, this pricey antiques shopping district offers over 150 stores and is great for browsing. *Address:* 78 avenue de Suffren and 54 de la Motte-Picquet (phone 43-06-69-90). *Hours:* Thur-Mon 10:30am-7pm. *Métro:* La Motte-Picquet/ Grenelle (6, 8, 10). *Bus:* 80.

Foyer de Grenelle

This small Protestant church has a continuous schedule of free classical music concerts. *Address:* 17 rue de l'Avre. *Métro:* La Motte-Picquet/Grenelle (6, 8, 10). *Buses:* 49, 80, 82.

Rue du Commerce

For a look at Paris as it was in the 1920's, take a walk down this street filled with quaint shops and inexpensive restaurants—a blue-collar/middle-class neighborhood still stuck in the past. At the street's south end, the grassy, narrow, two-blocks-long place du Commerce hosts free concerts on its bandstand during the summer. *Address:* between boulevard de Grenelle and rue Lakanal. *Métro:* Félix-Faure (8), Commerce (8), Avenue Émile Zola (10), La Motte-Picquet/Grenelle (6, 8, 10). *Buses:* 70, 80.

Rue de la Convention

One of the largest street markets (food, clothes, and other goods) in Paris lies on the south side of the 15th arrondissement. *Address:* on rue de la Convention, between rues Alain-Chartier and de Abbé-Groult. *Hours:* Tue, Thur, & Sun 8am-1pm & 4pm-7:30pm. *Métro:* Convention (12). *Buses:* 39, 49, 62.

Parc André Citroën

About a mile south of the Tour Eiffel along the Seine River, Paris's newest public park was built on the site of a former Citroën automobile factory. Its 34.6 acres feature over 2,000 trees, expansive grassy areas open for play (a rarity in Paris parks), and two large greenhouses with tropical and Mediter-ranean plants (open on weekends). *Address:* 214 rue St-Charles (phone 40-71-75-23). *Hours:* Sep 1-May 15: daily 8:30am-5:30pm; May 16-Aug 31: 8:30am-10pm. *Métro:* Place Baltard (8), Javel (10, C). *Buses:* 42, PC. *Admission:* free for park, 6F for greenhouses.

Parc Georges Brassens

Stuck in a neighborhood consisting primarily of block-style apartments and ugly urban planning, the Parc Georges Brassens is an oasis. It features a pretty pond with an old clock tower at its center, a garden of scented herbs for the blind, an artificial mountain stream, a tiny vineyard, merry-go-rounds, and a used book market (see below). The park's amusement-park look makes it one of the city's unique spots, seldom visited by tour-ists. *Address:* enter at place Jacques Marette (main entrance, north) off rue des Morillons, rue des Périchaux (southwest cor-ner), or rue Brancion (east). *Métro:* Convention (12), Porte de Versailles (12). *Buses:* 48, 89.

Marché du Livre Ancient et d'Occasion

Used and collectible books, some at extremely cheap prices, are sold in the sheds of the former horse market at Parc Georges Brassens. *Address:* rue Brancion side of park. *Hours:* Sat & Sun beginning at 9am and closing when vendors decide to quit. *Métro/Buses:* same as Parc Georges Brassens.

Parc des Expositions

On the south border of the arrondissement, straddling the boulevard Périphérique, a multiple-building exposition com-plex hosts weekly conventions and conferences, many of which have free or extremely cheap admission. Although they are geared to European business people, some of them (such as the annual auto, boat, and home furnishings shows) may be of interest to you. In the newspapers and weekly events publica-tions, they are listed under the *Salons et foires* and *Conferences* headings. You can also get information from any Office du Tourisme or a schedule of events from the Parc's information booth opposite the Métro station. *Address:* place de la Porte de Versailles. *Hours:* varies per event. *Métro:* Porte de Versailles (12). *Buses:* 39, 49, 58, 80, 89, PC.

16th Arrondissement

The narrow 16th arrondissement, bordered on two sides by the Seine River, is dominated by the Bois de Boulogne, the second-largest park in Paris. The park takes up the western half of the arrondissement and features numerous gardens, lakes, restaurants, and two horse-racing tracks on its grounds. The richest arrondissement in Paris, its posh neighborhoods feature elegant homes, shops, deluxe hotels, and celebrity restaurants, especially on the streets from the Arc de Triomphe to the Palais de Chaillot and in the former suburbs of Auteuil and Passy. You'll also find more museums in this arrondissement than anywhere else in the city.

The 16th arrondissement's boundaries are boulevards Richard Wallace, Maurice Barrès, and Maillot, avenue de Neuilly, place de la Maillot, Charles-de-Gaulle, and avenue de la Grande Armée (north), boulevards d'Auteuil, Anatole-France, and Périphérique (south), avenue Marceau and Seine River (east), and Seine River (west).

Palais de Chaillot

Built as a cultural center in the 1930's, the Palais de Chaillot is typical of the blocky, utilitarian architecture done in Paris between the two World Wars. Today, the building houses the Musée de la Marine, Musée des Monuments Français, Musée du Cinéma Henri Langlois (all below), Musée de l'Homme, Musée des Materiaux du CRMH, and Théatre National de Chaillot. From its central plaza (often dominated by skateboarders and rollerskaters) and the lower terrace lined with dazzling fountains (especially at night) are some of the best views of the Tour Eiffel across the Seine River. *Address:* 17 place du Trocadéro. *Hours:* see individual sights below. *Métro:* Trocadéro (6, 9). *Buses:* 22, 30, 32, 63, 72, 82. *Admission:* Plaza, terrace, & adjoining park are free; see individual listings for other prices.

Musée de la Marine

The naval history museum of France exhibits model ships, weapons, documents, drawings, and other artifacts from the 17th century to the present day. *Address:* Palais de Chaillot (phone 45-53-31-70). Hours: Wed-Mon 9:45am-5:15pm. *Métro/Buses:* same as Palais de Chaillot. *Admission:* Carte Musées et Monuments.

Musée des Monuments Français

If you think you'll never have enough time to see all the great sights and monuments in France, then visit this interesting museum created by architect/restorationist Viollet-le-Duc in 1882. It contains reproductions of all the major works of sculpture, monuments, medieval frescoes, and murals found in France, plus models of the great Gothic churches and other important architecture. *Address:* Palais de Chaillot (phone 44-05-39-10). *Hours:* Wed-Mon 10am-6pm. *Métro/Buses:* same as Palais de Chaillot. *Admission:* 21F, Carte Musées et Monuments.

Musée du Cinema Henri Langlois

The history of film from the Lumière brothers to the present is presented through this museum's collection of posters, photographs, manuscripts, costumes, and cameras. There's also a film studio. *Address:* Palais de Chaillot (phone 45-53-21-86). *Hours:* guided tours (only) Wed-Sun at 10am, 11am, 2pm, 3pm, 4pm, 5pm. *Métro/Buses:* same as Palais de Chaillot. *Admission:* Carte Musées et Monuments.

Musée des Materiaux—Centre de Recherche Sur Les Monuments Historiques

This combination of museum and research center shows the variety of building materials used in historical monuments. Scale models of famous buildings and types of foundations and frameworks are displayed. *Address:* 9 avenue Albert de Munin in east wing of Palais de Chaillot (phone 47-27-84-64). *Hours:* by appointment only. *Métro/Buses:* same as Palais de Chaillot.

Cimetière de Passy

This small cemetery, across the street behind the Palais de Chaillot, holds the graves of composer Claude Debussy and painter Édouard Manet, a precursor and supporter of the radical Impressionists. *Address:* 2 rue du Commandant-Schloesing. *Métro:* Trocadéro (6, 9). *Buses:* 22, 30, 32, 63.

Musée d'Art Moderne de la Ville de Paris
Housed in the east wing of the large and modern Palais de Tokyo is an outstanding collection of modern and contemporary art owned by the city of Paris. Often overlooked by tourists who head for the more popular Centre Georges Pompidou, this collection features paintings and sculpture by Gris, Léger, both Delaunays, Picasso, Braque, Matisse, Chagall, and many others. There are also good Bourdelle sculptures outside. Several temporary exhibitions focusing on various schools of modern art are held here annually (expensive). Jazz concerts run here two nights a month. *Address:* 11 avenue du Président-Wilson (phone 53-67-40-00). *Hours:* Tue-Thur & Fri 10am-5:30pm, Sat & Sun 10am-7pm. *Métro:* Alma-Marceau (C), Iéna (9). *Buses:* 32, 42, 63, 72, 80, 82, 92. *Admission:* Carte Musées et Monuments; jazz concerts vary in price.

Palais de l'Image et du Son (includes Centre
National de la Photographie & Cinémathèque Française)
The newest museum in Paris is an amalgamation of several photographic, film, and audio-visual collections that have been scattered across the city for several years. Housed in the west wing of the Palais de Tokyo, the museum includes the Cinémathèque Française (formerly in the Palais de Chaillot), which shows two different films each week. *Address:* 13 avenue du Président-Wilson (phone 47-23-61-27). *Hours:* Wed 10am-8:30pm, Thur-Mon 10am-5:40pm. *Métro/Buses:* same as Musée d'Art Moderne. *Admission:* 30F for photography museum and viewing of two movies (a great bargain, considering the cost of movies in Paris).

Musée des Arts Asiatiques Guimet
The national museum of Asian art, founded in 1879 by Lyon industrialist Emile Guimet to house his collection of Oriental antiques and later nationalized as a part of the Musée du Louvre's Far East collection, is a major research center on Asian culture. Over 50,000 works of art, sculpture, and other items are displayed in several galleries. The adjoining annex, Galeries du Panthéon Boudhique du Japon et de la Chine (19 avenue

d'Iéna), focuses on Buddhism, with 300 paintings and 600 statues. *Address:* 6 place d'Iéna (phone 47-23-61-65). *Hours:* Wed-Mon 9:45am-6pm. *Métro:* Iéna (9). *Buses:* 22, 32, 63, 82. *Admission:* 18F on Sundays, Carte Musées et Monuments.

Goethe Institute
This well-organized German cultural organization, with locations in major cities throughout the world, offers a variety of free and inexpensive activities. Its art and photography exhibitions are usually quite good, and it has several films and conferences each month. *Address:* 17 avenue d'Iéna (phone 44-43-92-30). *Hours:* Mon-Fri 1am-8pm. *Métro:* Iéna (9). *Buses:* 32, 63, 82.

Fondation Gulbenkian & Centre Culturel Portuguais
The Portuguese cultural center and adjoining foundation host many free art exhibitions. *Address:* 51 avenue d'Iéna (phone 47-20-86-84). *Hours:* Mon-Sat 9am-12:30pm & 2pm-6pm. *Métro:* Iéna (9), Kléber (6). *Buses:* 22, 30, 92.

Musée Dapper
Traditional art and other objects from pre-colonial Africa are the focus in this small museum. *Address:* 50 avenue Victor-Hugo (phone 45-00-01-50). *Hours:* daily 11am-7pm. *Métro:* Victor Hugo (2), Avenue Foch (C). *Buses:* 52, 82. *Admission:* 20F.

Musée Arménien de France & Musée d'Ennery
On the ground floor of a Napoléon III-style mansion, the Musée Arménien de France celebrates the culture of Armenia from the 8th century to the early 20th century through 3,000 art objects and historical documents. The Musée d'Ennery upstairs offers a surprising collection of over 6,000 items illustrating daily life and beliefs in China and Japan. It includes dolls, paintings, *netsukes*, statues, jade perfume bottles, masks, and documents. *Address:* 59 avenue Foch (phone 45-56-15-88 & 45-53-57-96). *Hours:* Musée Arménien de France: Thur & Sun 2pm-6pm; Musée d'Ennery: Thur & Sun 2pm-5pm; both museums closed in August. *Métro:* Port Dauphine (2), Avenue Foch (C), Victor Hugo (2). *Buses:* 82, PC.

Musée de la Contrefaçon
Founded in 1951 by the Union of Manufacturers, this one-room museum discusses the crime of forgery and counterfeiting from

the Roman era to the present. Its exhibits include imitation products, labels, perfume, and money. (Are you sure that's a Rolex you bought from the street vendor yesterday?) *Address:* 16 rue de la Faisanderie (phone 45-01-51-11). *Hours:* Mon & Wed 2pm-4:30pm, Fri 9:30am-noon. *Métro:* Porte Dauphine (2), Avenue Foch (C). *Buses:* 52, PC. *Admission:* 10F.

Porte Dauphine Métro Entrance
The Porte Dauphine Métro station entrance (line 2), with its sweeping glass canopy and green, wrought-iron supports, is the best example in Paris of the art nouveau Métro entrances created by architect Hector Guimard during the early 1900's. It's only one of two left with the glass roof intact. (The other is at the Abbesses station in the 18th arrondissement.) Guimard died in New York in 1942, the same year a Nazi officer was shot by a Resistance member while exiting this station. *Address:* avenue Foch at boulevard Flandrin. *Buses:* PC.

Jardin de Ranelagh
The Jardin de Ranelagh, located across the street from the pricey Musée Marmottan (largest depository in Paris for Monet paintings), is a large, triangular park intersected by several streets. It features an old-style carrousel that both adults and children will enjoy. *Address:* avenue du Ranelagh & avenue Raphaël. *Métro:* La Muette (9), Boucainvilliers (C), Ranelagh (9). *Buses:* 22, 32, 52. *Admission:* 5F for carrousel.

Musée de Radio France
Housed in the modern, round building of France's state broadcasting company, this museum exhibits models, machines, and documents about the history of radio and television in France. Regular classical music concerts are held in its auditorium. *Address:* 116 avenue du Président-Kennedy (phone 42-30-33-83). *Hours:* guided tours: Mon-Sat at 10:30am, 11:30am, 2:30pm, 3:30pm, 4:30pm. *Métro:* Kennedy-Radio France (C). *Buses:* 22, 52, 70, 72. *Admission:* 15F for museum and tour, free or extremely cheap for concerts.

Statue of Liberty
Opposite Radio France on a long, narrow island in the Seine River, there's a small copy of America's Statue of Liberty. From the manmade island, you can get good views of the Tour Eiffel,

Radio France, and the river traffic. *Address:* Allée des Cygnes; steps lead down to the island from the Pont de Grenelle (connects quai de Grenelle to avenue du Président-Kennedy). *Métro:* Kennedy-Radio France (C), Bir-Hakeim (6, C). *Buses:* 70, 72.

Maison de Balzac

Honoré de Balzac wrote the last part of his book *Comédie Humaine* here, his last and only surviving residence in Paris (1840-47). Today, his home is an educational center for the study of his literature and a museum with exhibits of his books, portraits, furniture, and belongings. *Address:* 47 rue Raynouard (down a flight of stairs into a garden) (phone 42-24-56-38). *Hours:* Tue-Sun 10am-5:40pm. *Métro:* Passy (6), Kennedy-Radio France (C). *Buses:* 32, 72. *Admission:* 17.5F, Carte Musées et Monuments.

Passy

From the Maison de Balzac, follow the narrow rue de l'Annonciation into the heart of the former suburb of Passy (a middle/upper class neighborhood). Along the way, you'll pass a church on a quiet square, which is contrasted one block further by a noisy street market, its boisterous vendors hawking food and other products. At the end of the street is the covered market **Marché de Passy**, where locals buy fresh fish, meat, and produce, get their shoes repaired, and purchase watches and other products. For a slice of modern Passy, veer to the right across small place de Passy to rue Passy, where you'll find chic boutiques and other interesting stores for window shopping. *Address:* triangular area between rues de l'Annonciation, Passy, & Raynouard. *Métro:* Passy (6), La Muette (9). *Bus:* 32.

Fondation Le Corbusier & Villa La Roche

A small collection of furniture and art of the famed Swiss architect Le Corbusier (1887-1969) is exhibited in the Villa La Roche, the first private house he had built in Paris (1923). The Cubist design of the pedestal elevated house with minimal decoration represents his architectural style well. The headquarters and research library of the Fondation Le Corbusier are housed in the adjoining Villa Jeanneret, which has an extensive microfilm collection of the architect's designs, notes, and drawings. *Address:* 10 square du Docteur Blanche (phone 42-88-41-53).

Hours: Fondation Le Corbusier: Mon-Fri 9am-12:30pm & 1:30pm-6pm; Villa La Roche: Mon-Thur 10am-12:30pm & 1:30pm-6pm, Fri 10am-12:30pm & 1:30pm-5pm; closed Dec 25-Jan 1 and August. *Métro:* Jasmin (9). *Buses:* 22, 32, 52, PC. *Admission:* free for Villa Jeanneret, 15F for Villa La Roche.

Bois de Boulogne
The second-largest park (2,200 acres) in Paris is home to many sights (see below), plus hiking trails, stadiums, lakes, a bicycle path, and a few outstanding restaurants. You can wander through the park any time, though avoid it at night, since it's a hub for drug dealers, prostitutes, and other unsavory characters. Specific park attractions are described below. *Address:* enter off boulevards Richard-Wallace, Maurice-Barrès & Maillot (north), boulevards d'Auteuil & Anatole-France (south), or boulevards Suchet, Lannes, & l'Amiral Bruix (east). The west side of the park is bordered by the Seine River. *Hours:* open 24 hours. *Métro:* Les Sablons (1), Porte Maillot (1, C), Port Dauphiné (2), Avenue Foch (C), Avenue Henri Martin (C), Ranelagh (9), La Muette (9), Porte d'Auteuil (10). *Buses:* 32, 43, 52, 63, 73, 82, 244, PC (to or near its boundaries). *Admission:* park is free; some sights charge a fee.

Jardin d'Acclimation, Musée en Herbe, & Théâtre du Jardin
At the north end of the Bois de Boulogne, there's an amusement park, zoo, theater, and art museum designed primarily for children. A miniature train runs to these sights from Porte Maillot. *Address:* boulevard des Sablons entrance (phone 40-67-97-66). *Hours:* Sun-Fri 10am-6pm; Sat 2pm-6pm. *Métro:* Les Sablons (1). *Buses:* 73. *Admission:* 16F for museum, 9F for amusement park, 6F for train, free classical music concerts at theater.

Musée des Arts et Traditions Populaires
This museum focuses on French ethnology from the 18th to the 20th centuries, with exhibits on agriculture, domestic life, religious worship, folk art, and much more. *Address:* 6 avenue du Mahatma-Gandhi, next to Jardin d'Acclimation (phone 44-17-60-00). *Hours:* Wed-Mon 9:45am-5:15pm; closed May 1. *Métro/Buses:* same as Jardin d'Acclimation. *Admission:* 20F, Carte Musées et Monuments.

Château de Bagatelle & Parc de Bagatelle

On a 60-acre section of the Bois de Boulogne (west side), you'll find a small château constructed in 1777 by the Count of Artois for Queen Marie Antoinette and a beautiful park featuring a variety of gardens. There are good views of the Seine River and Ile du Puteaux from the château's terrace. Concerts and other events are held regularly in the park. *Address:* Route de Sèvres (phone 40-67-97-00). *Hours:* park: daily 8:30am-8pm; château: expensive guided tours on weekends. *Métro/Buses:* Pont de Neuilly (1) plus bus 43, Porte Maillot (1, C) plus bus 244, Porte d'Auteuil (10) plus bus 244N. *Admission:* park is free on Sunday, 6F other days; concerts vary in price.

Jardin de Shakespeare

All of the plants mentioned in the plays of William Shakespeare are grown in a small garden in the Bois de Boulogne's Pré Catelan area. *Address:* near intersection of allées de Longchamp & de la Reine Marguerite. *Hours:* daily 7:30am-8pm. *Métro/ Buses:* Porte Maillot (1, C) plus bus 244. *Admission:* 3F.

Hippodromes Longchamp & d'Auteuil

Feeling lucky? The Bois de Boulogne has two horse tracks. Longchamp is the setting for the prestigious annual Grand Prix races—gala events similar to the American Triple Crown. Auteuil features steeplechase-style racing. You can enter both tracks for a relatively low price, except during the annual races, when all seats are reserved far in advance. *Address:* south corners of Bois de Boulogne (Auteuil phone 42-24-47-04, Longchamp phone 42-24-13-29). *Hours:* check newspaper sports pages for race times. *Métro:* Longchamp: Boulogne Jean Jaurès (10) plus bus 244N; d'Auteuil: Porte d'Auteuil (10). *Buses:* d'Auteuil: 32, 52, 244N, PC. *Admission:* 25F for cheapest seats.

Jardin des Serres d'Auteuil

Across from the Bois de Boulogne in the southwest corner of Paris, several greenhouses grow the plants and flowers used in the city's municipal buildings. Surrounding the greenhouses in a park-like setting are terraced flower gardens, trees, shrubs, benches, and a stone retaining wall containing pillars decorated with 14 Rodin medallions. *Address:* 3 avenue de la Porte d'Auteuil. *Hours:* daily 10am-5:30pm. *Métro/Buses:* same as Hippodrome d'Auteuil. *Admission:* 3F.

Square des Poètes

Next to the Jardin des Serres d'Auteuil, a park features the busts of 48 French poets and writers, including Molière, Lamartine, Hugo, Baudelaire, Rimbaud, and Verlaine. *Address:* enter off avenues du Géneral-Sarail or de la Porte d'Auteuil. *Métro/ Buses:* same as Hippodrome d'Auteuil.

Parc des Princes

This is the largest stadium in Paris, accommodating 50,000 people for soccer (called "football" in France), rugby, and other sports. *Address:* 24 rue du Commandant-Guilbaud. *Hours:* check newspaper sports pages. *Métro:* Porte de St-Cloud (9). *Buses:* 22, 52, 62, 72, PC. *Admission:* extremely cheap seats are available for some events.

Musée National du Sport

Over 150 years of sports history is documented in this small museum housed in the Parc des Princes stadium. Temporary exhibits cover a variety of sports themes. *Address:* same as Parc des Princes (phone 40-45-99-12). *Hours:* Mon-Fri 9:30am-12:30pm & 2pm-5pm, Sat 9:30am-6pm. *Métro/Buses:* same as Parc des Princes. *Admission:* 20F.

17th Arrondissement

The 17th arrondissement in the northwest corner of Paris is primarily residential. Divided by the train tracks from the Gare St-Lazare, the southern half is an extension of the upper-middle-class 8th and 16th arrondissements. North of the tracks in the former village of Batignolles, the area gets poorer and more industrial. Except for the Palais des Congrés, a good art museum, and a few street markets, this area is fairly dull for the traveler.

The boundaries of the 17th arrondissement are boulevard Périphérique (north and west), avenue de Neuilly, places de la Maillot and Charles-de-Gaulle, and boulevard de la Grande Armée (south), and boulevards Wagram, de Courcelles, and des Batignolles and avenues Clichy and de St-Ouen (east).

Palais des Congrés de Paris
The huge Paris convention center complex features a multi-level shopping mall with over 100 stores, a large hotel, an Air France bus stop (for CDG airport), and numerous conferences and trade shows, some of which are free to the public. Check with the information desk for a current schedule. *Address:* 2 place de la Porte Maillot (phone 40-68-22-39). *Hours:* 9am-8pm for most stores; convention hours vary. *Métro:* Porte Maillot (1, C). *Buses:* 73, 82, 244, PC, Air France.

Rue Poncelet & Place des Ternes
One of the best food markets in west Paris operates on the narrow rue Poncelet, where you'll also find a good *charcuterie* (deli, ready-to-go foods) and *patisserie* (pastry shop). A few steps away at place des Ternes, there's an active flower and plant market, plus the remains of an art nouveau-style Métro entrance. *Address:* both off avenue des Ternes. *Hours:* Tue-Sun 8am-7:30pm. *Métro:* Ternes (2). *Buses:* 30, 31, 43, 93, 93.

Musée Jean-Jacques Henner

Self-portraits and hundreds of drawings and paintings show the Alsatian painter's propensity for the nude female figure. The collection is housed in an 1865 mansion in a neighborhood that offers a good look at mid to late 19th-century Paris architecture. *Address:* 43 avenue de Villiers (phone 47-63-42-73). *Hours:* Tue-Sun 10am-noon & 2pm-5pm. *Métro:* Malesherbes (3). *Buses:* 30, 31, 94. *Admission:* 15F, Carte Musées et Monuments.

Square des Batignolles

This large park, an oasis in a warehouse district and blue-collar area long past its prime, features several flower gardens and some interesting statues, including one resembling a priest gargling and strangling a bird at the same time at the center of a pond . On the south side of the park, you can watch trains from the Gare St-Lazare. *Address:* enter off place Charles-Fillion (north), rue des Moines (east), or rue Cardinet (west). *Métro:* Brochant (13). *Buses:* 31, 54, 66.

Rue des Moines & Cité des Fleurs

These long parallel streets (three blocks apart) offer unique contrasts in this arrondissement. Rue des Moines travels through a working-class section often seen in movies, with crowded neighborhood bars, food markets, and boisterous residents. Meanwhile, Cité des Fleurs is a subdued residential street of middle-class homes, courtyards, and private gardens. *Address:* between avenue de Clichy & rue de la Jonquière. *Métro:* Brochant (13). *Buses:* 31, 54, 66, 74.

18th Arrondissement

The 18th arrondissement encompasses the former village of Montmartre, a quarter popularized by late 19th-century artists through their paintings of the area. Since then, artists have gone there to live and paint, including the modern artists Braque, Dufy, Matisse, and Picasso. Though a few artists still work in the area, Montmartre is known today for the numerous tourist traps and overpriced restaurants surrounding its primary sight, the Basilique du Sacré Cœur. If you can overlook those, however, the narrow, twisting streets of the 18th are fun to explore, and there are a few good museums for rainy days. The rest of the arrondissement is less desirable, with the notorious Pigalle area on the south border and poor immigrant neighborhoods dominating the eastern half.

The 18th arrondissement's boundaries are boulevard Périphérique (north), boulevards de Clichy, Rochechouart, and de la Chapelle (S), rue d'Aubervilliers (east), and avenues de Clichy and St-Ouen (west).

Basilique du Sacré Cœur

Built from 1873 to 1914, the domed cathedral and Paris landmark (it's what you see first when entering Paris from the north) looks more like a Turkish mosque than the Gothic churches associated with France. It's built on the highest point in Paris, and you can climb several steps up a spiral staircase to the top of its dome for a panoramic view. (There are also good views of Paris to the south from its steps and terrace.) While the church is dark and solemn inside, there's a constant carnival outside aided by street performers, artists, musicians, and other vendors who camp on the steps. If you hate crowds, come here early. *Address:* place du Parvis du Sacré Cœur (phone 42-51-17-02).

Hours: sanctuary: daily 6:45am-11pm; dome & crypt: summer: daily 9am-7pm; winter: 9am-6pm. *Métro:* Anvers (2), Abbesses (12). *Buses:* 30, 54, 80, 85, Montmartrobus. *Admission:* free for sanctuary, 15F for dome and crypt.

Église St-Pierre-de-Montmartre
This small Gothic church, dedicated in 1147 and built on the site of a Roman temple, is only a few steps west of the Basilique du Sacré Cœur. Its interior features black marble columns, two 17th-century paintings, and 27 stained glass windows (from 1952) that depict the crucifixion and scenes from the lives of the saints. *Address:* 2 rue du Mont Cenis. *Métro/Buses:* same as Basilique du Sacré Cœur.

Place du Tertre
The cafés on and near this small square were hangouts of the Impressionists and the artists who followed them at the turn of the century. Today, it's a tourist trap, where crowds of ignorant travelers buy tacky paintings of Montmartre scenes at exorbitant prices and leave Paris thinking they've discovered a master French artist. The best thing here: the free map of other Montmartre sights, available at Place du Tertre's own tourist office. *Address:* off rue du Mont Cenis, via rue Norvins. *Métro:* Abbesses (12). *Buses:* Montmartrobus (neighborhood bus).

Chapelle du Martyre
This 19th-century chapel lies over the spot where St. Denis, the first Bishop of Paris, was beheaded in 250 A.D. by the Romans. According to legend, St. Denis carried his head for miles, dropping it on the present site of the Cathédrale St-Denis (see *Paris Suburbs* chapter). It's also the place where St. Ignatius Loyola and St. Francis Xavier founded the Jesuits in 1534. *Address:* 9 rue Yvonne-Le-Tac. *Métro/Buses:* same as Abbesses Métro.

Bateau-Lavoir
From their studios in an old piano factory on this site, Picasso, Braque, and Gris invented Cubism in the early 1920's. Although the original building burned down a few years ago, the new structure is still used for artist studios, and most are happy to show you their work. *Address:* place Émile-Goudeau. *Métro/Buses:* same as Abbesses Métro Station.

Artists

There are many artists' studios spread throughout Montmartre, including the large Cité International des Arts building (avenue Junot), which the city leases to international artists. Although many studios have *Interdit* (No Trespassing) signs on their doors, some artists, upon a polite request (it helps to speak French), will gladly show you their work and sell you some, too.

Pigalle

En route to Montmartre, you may pass through Pigalle, the sordid red light district of Paris. It's relatively safe during the day, when most of the prostitutes, transvestites, drug dealers, and such aren't working. But enter at your own risk at night. *Métro:* Blanche (2), Pigalle (2, 12), Anvers (2), place Clichy (2, 13). *Buses:* 30, 54, 67, 68, Montmartrobus.

Tati

Yet another location for the frantic discount department chain (see listing in the 6th arrondissement chapter). *Address:* 2-30 boulevard Rochechouart. *Métro:* Barbès-Rochechouart (2, 4). *Buses:* 30, 31, 54, 56, 85.

Moulin Rouge

The famed dance hall, built in 1885 and immortalized in Toulouse-Lautrec's paintings, still boasts its landmark red windmill over the main entrance. Like the other revues in town, it's very expensive, so take a photograph of the windmill and head for cheaper sights. *Address:* 82 boulevard de Clichy. *Métro:* Blanche (2). *Buses:* 30, 54, 68, 74, 80.

Rue Lepic

Away from the crowds (except during the annual antique auto race held on the second Sunday in October), this long and winding cobblestone street offers a good glimpse of residential Montmartre. Vincent Van Gogh lived with his brother Théodore at #54. *Address:* between place Blanche & rue Norvins. *Métro:* Blanche (2), Abbesses (12). *Buses:* 30, 54, 68, 74, 80, Montmartrobus.

Moulin de la Galette & Moulin Radet

Only two windmills are left from several built in Montmartre over six centuries ago. The garden next to the Moulin de la

The Abbesses Métro entrance in the Montmartre neighborhood is one of only two entrances designed by Hector Guimard left in Paris that still have the original glass canopy.

Galette is where Renoir painted several of his Paris scenes. *Address:* 79 rue Lepic. *Métro:* Abbesses (12), Lamarck-Caulaincourt (12). *Buses:* 80, Montmartrobus.

Abbesses Métro Entrance

The entrance of the Abbesses Métro station (line 12)—with its glass canopy, decorated wrought-iron supports, and orange-tongued lanterns—is one of the prettiest in Paris and one of two Métro stations left in Paris with its original glass roof. (The other is at Port Dauphine.) It's also the deepest Métro station: 300 feet below street level, 285 steps down an artistically painted stairwell to the train platform. Tourists often use the elevator. *Address:* place des Abbesses. *Buses:* Montmartrobus.

Square Suzanne-Buisson

Named after the most famous female Resistance fighter, this small park offers good views of the windmills, as well as a sunken *boules* court and a statue of St. Denis clutching his head to his breast. *Address:* entrance off place des Quatre Frères Casadesus. *Métro/Buses:* same as Moulin de la Galette.

Cimetière Montmartre

Many famous Parisians rest in the Montmartre cemetery. The most notable and interesting tombs are those of German author/poet Heinrich Heine, novelists Alexandre Dumas, Émile Zola, and Henri Beyle (better known as Stendhal), artists Degas, Fragonard, and Ary Scheffer, filmmaker François Truffault, dancer Nijinsky, and composers Hector Berlioz and Jacques Offenbach. *Address:* avenue Rachel; stairs lead down to this street from the rue Caulaincourt bridge. *Métro:* place Clichy (2, 13), Blanche (2), La Fourche (13). *Buses:* 30, 54, 74, 80, 95.

Montmartre Vineyard

The only commercial vineyard in Paris lies on a hill opposite the famed Lapin Agile Cabaret. Although it's an unexceptional wine (famous mainly for its diuretic qualities; a 17th-century proverb states, "With wine from Montmartre, drink a pint and you urinate a quart"), the Montmartre community hosts a fun festival the first Saturday in October to celebrate the new vintage. *Address:* corner of rues des Saules & Vincent. *Métro:* Lamarck-Caulaincourt (12). *Buses:* 80, Montmartrobus. *Admission:* get permission from the caretaker or arrondissement Secrétariat Générale (1 place Jules Joffrin) to go inside.

Cimetière St-Vincent

Behind the tall, ivy-covered walls across from the Lapin Agile is a small cemetery whose most famous internee is the artist Maurice Utrillo, best known for his paintings of 19th-century Montmartre. *Address:* 6 rue Lucien Gaulard. *Métro/Buses:* same as Montmartre Vineyard.

Utrillo Paintings

When Utrillo died in 1955, he left two of his paintings as a gift to the 18th arrondissement government. *Address:* 1 place Jules-Joffrin. *Métro:* Jules-Joffrin (12). *Buses:* 31, 60, 80, 85. *Admission:* free, but get permission from the Secrétariat Générale.

Musée Placard Erik Satie

This is the smallest museum in Paris—a single room exhibiting the scores of composer Erik Satie. *Address:* 6 rue Cortot (phone 42-78-15-18). *Hours:* Mon-Sun, by appointment only. *Métro/Buses:* same as Montmartre Vineyard.

Goutte d'Or

The Goutte d'Or, on the east side of the arrondissement (west of the Gare du Nord tracks), is an immigrant ghetto inhabited primarily by North Africans. During the day, its shops, with their African and Arabic character, are interesting, but be cautious. And don't go there at night. This area has one of the worst reputations for crime in the city. *Address:* approximate boundaries are rue Ordener (north), boulevard de la Chapelle (south), Gare du Nord train lines (east), & boulevard Barbès (west). *Métro:* La Chapelle (2), Barbès-Rochechouart (2, 4), Château Rouge (4), Marcadet Poissonniers (4, 12). *Buses:* 30, 31, 54, 56, 60, 85.

Villa Poissonnière

If you're in the above area, check out this group of Louis-Philippe-style townhouses, some with exteriors covered entirely by tiles. *Address:* between rues de la Goutte d'Or & Polonceau. *Métro:* La Chapelle (2), Barbès-Rochechouart (2, 4). *Buses:* 31, 56.

19th Arrondissement

The 19th arrondissement is primarily a blue-collar, industrial area. Today, to revitalize the district, old buildings and warehouses are being razed and turned into new businesses. The best creation at the arrondissement's north end is the Cité des Sciences et de l'Industrie, a science/industry museum and entertainment complex. The Parc de Buttes-Chaumont, on the south end of the arrondissement, has a pretty lake and hilltop views of Paris.

The boundaries of the 19th arrondissement are boulevard Périphérique (north and east), rue de Belleville (south), and rues d'Aubervilliers and de la Villette (west).

Parc de la Villette

The old slaughterhouse district of La Villette, a 75-acre section of canal-intersected land, was turned into a park and multi-use complex about 10 years ago. Today, it's home to the Cité des Sciences et de l'Industrie (see below), Cité de la Musique/ Musée de la Musique (221 avenue Jean-Jaurès), Conservatoire National Supérieur de Musique et de Danse de Paris (the national academy for music, theater, and dance, with occasional free recitals), Grande Halle (exhibition/convention space converted from a former Baltard pavilion), Zenith (an inflatable rock concert auditorium identified by a diving red airplane on a concrete pedestal), and Théâtre Paris Villette. *Address:* enter off avenues Jean-Jaurès or Corentin-Cariou, or boulevard MacDonald. *Hours:* park open 24 hours; hours for organizations vary. *Métro:* Corentin-Cariou (7), Porte de la Villette (7), Porte de Pantin (5). *Buses:* 60, 75, PC. *Admission:* park is free; admission varies for each organization.

Navette de la Villette

Take a 30-minute guided boat tour of the canals surrounding the La Villette complex. *Address:* 5 bis quai de la Loire. *Hours:* daily 10:30am–7pm. *Métro:* Jaurès (2, 5, 7b), Laumière (5). *Buses:* 26, 60. *Admission:* 20F.

Club Alpin Français

There are free lectures, movies, slide shows, and lots of interesting people at the weekly meeting of the national mountain climbing club (Ile de France chapter). *Address:* 24 avenue Laumière (phone 42-02-75-94). *Hours:* Thur 8pm-midnight. *Métro:* Laumière (5). *Buses:* 60.

Rotonde de la Villette

Set in an open space overlooking the Basin de la Villette canal, the Roman-inspired Rotonde de la Villette was a toll house built in 1789 to guard the road from Flanders and north Germany. A short distance south, straddling the 10th arrondissement border, is an unusual elevated Métro line (2) on iron and stone pillars. *Address:* place Stalingrad. *Métro:* Stalingrad (2, 5, 7), Jaurès (2, 5, 7b). *Buses:* 26, 60.

Parc des Buttes-Chaumont

The crescent-shaped, woodsy Parc des Buttes-Chaumont, often avoided by tourists due to its backwater location, is worth a visit. Laid out in 1864 by Baron Haussmann on a former quarry, its hilly 60 acres feature a waterfall, a large lake crossed by a suspension bridge, a tiny neoclassical temple atop a craggy hill, crisscrossing trails, an artificial grotto, and three restaurants. As the second-highest location in Paris, it offers good views of the city (if you make the climb to the temple), and there are free concerts from its bandstand during the summer. *Address:* enter off rue Manin (north and west), rue Botzaris (south), or rue Crimée (east). *Métro:* Botzaris (7b), Buttes Chaumont (7b). *Buses:* 60, 75.

Cité des Sciences et de l'Industrie

This is the scientific answer to the artsy Centre Georges Pompidou, with lots of glass, exposed duct work, ultra-modern facilities, and an avant-garde style. As the largest science and industry museum in France, it emphasizes a "hands-on, viewer participation" approach with innovative exhibits to illustrate the

The giant chrome ball La Géode dominates the grounds of the Cité des Sciences et de l'Industrie. The movie theater inside La Géode is the museum's most popular sight.

greatest scientific/technological achievements in the world. Conferences offering additional information about scientific topics are presented in the 1,000-seat auditorium. However, its most popular feature is **La Géode**, a gigantic chrome ball set in a pond in front of the main building. Inside the ball, there's a movie theater with a 1,000-square-meter hemispheric screen— an incredible cinematic experience. Children will find special exhibits and workshops, and in the park they'll enjoy touring the submarine sitting next to La Géode and whisking down a gigantic dragon slide made from recycled pipes. The Cité has its own restaurant and money exchange, and there are two modern hotels across the canal. *Address:* 30 avenue Corentin Cariou (phone 40-05-70-00). *Hours:* Tue-Sun 10am-6pm. *Métro/Buses:* same as Parc de la Villette. *Admission:* Carte Musées et Monuments; slide is free.

20th Arrondissement

On the east side of Paris, the 20th arrondissement is the true melting pot of the city, a largely residential area where you'll find a high percentage of Paris's immigrant population. Since the French Revolution, refugees seeking asylum and work in Paris have settled in this district. For a world cultural experience, walk through its streets during the day, where you will hear Arabic, Russian, Greek, Polish, and many other languages. Its only major sight is the Père Lachaise Cemetery, featuring the graves of many famous French and a few Americans.

The 20th arrondissement's boundaries are rue de Belleville (north), cours de Vincennes (south), boulevard Périphérique (east), and boulevards de Belleville, de Ménilmontant, and de Charonne (west).

Belleville
The north part of the 20th arrondissement is the former village of Belleville, a traditional working-class district now inhabited primarily by immigrants. Interspersed between modern shops, foreign restaurants, and utilitarian apartment buildings are Old World *passages* and interesting side streets called *villas*, usually containing 19th-century row houses built on cul-de-sacs. *Address:* approximate boundaries are rue de Belleville (north), rue de Ménilmontant (south), avenue Gambetta (east), & boulevard de Belleville (west). *Métro:* Belleville (2, 11), Pyrénées (11), Jourdain (11), Télégraphe (11), Porte des Lilas (3b, 11), St-Fargeau (3b), Couronnes (2). *Buses:* 26, 60, 96.

Parc de Belleville
Less than a mile south of Parc des Buttes-Chaumont, the modern Parc de Belleville (opened 1988) offers terraced flower gar-

dens and artificial waterfalls that cascade down its hilly terrain. From the rue Piat bordering the park's north end, there are good views of east Paris. *Address:* enter off rue Piat (north), rue des Couronnes (south), rue Botha (east), or rue Julien Lacroix (west). *Métro:* Pyrénées (11). *Buses:* 26, 96.

Ménilmontant

The former village of Ménilmontant, located in the middle of the arrondissement, is similar in character to Belleville, with many *villas, passages,* and immigrant residents. *Address:* approximate boundaries are rue de Ménilmontant (north), avenue Gambetta (south), boulevard Mortier (east), and boulevard de Ménilmontant (west). *Métro:* Ménilmontant (2), St-Fargeau (3b), Père Lachaise (2, 3), Gambetta (3, 3b), Pelleport (3b), Porte de Bagnolet (3). *Buses:* 26, 60, 96.

Église Notre-Dame-de-la-Croix

This church, the largest in the arrondissement, features regular free classical music concerts. *Address:* 2 rue Julien Lacroix. *Métro:* Ménilmontant (2). *Buses:* 96.

Cimetière du Père Lachaise

This is the largest and most famous cemetery in Paris, and rightly so. Its list of interred souls is a who's who of famous French, Europeans, and even a few Americans. Begun in 1804 and named after a Jesuit priest who had a country home at the site of the present chapel, the cemetery is a maze of streets, with monuments and graves piled nearly atop each other. The most famous tombs are those of artists Corot, David, Daumier, Delacroix, Ingres, Modigliani, Pissarro, and Seurat; photographer Nadar; Gertrude Stein (who held court for Picasso, Hemingway, and other cultural greats of the 1920's); urban planners Baron Haussmann and Bienvenüe (who built the Métro); composers and musicians Chopin, Bizet, Piaf; American rocker Jim Morrison; writers Balzac, La Fontaine, Molière, Proust, Apollinaire, Collette, and Wilde; architect Visconti; and actresses Sarah Bernhardt and Simone Signoret. Among the 116 acres of monuments and tombs, there's also a memorial to the tragic 12th-century lovers Abelard and Héloïse and a monument to 147 street fighters executed here by firing squad during the 1871 Commune uprising. Simply put, this cemetery is a Paris must.

Address: enter off boulevard de Ménilmontant (main entrance), avenue Gambetta (north), rue de la Reunion (south), or rue des Rondeaux (east). *Hours:* Sun 9am-6pm, Mon-Fri 8am-6pm, & Sat 8:30am-6pm. *Métro:* Père Lachaise (2, 3), Philippe Auguste (2), Gambetta (3, 3b). *Buses:* 26, 60, 61, 69, 76. *Admission:* free. At the main entrance, you can buy a detailed cemetery map showing the location of celebrity tombs for 10F.

Marché aux Puces de la Porte de Montreuil

Near the southeast corner of the arrondissement, a large flea market features extremely cheap secondhand clothes, some antiques, tools, appliances, and other "junque." It gets even cheaper on Monday, when dealers want to reduce their inventory. *Address:* Porte de Montreuil. *Hours:* Sat-Mon 6:30am-7:30pm. *Métro:* Porte de Montreuil (9). *Buses:* PC, 351 (stop on your way to CDG).

Paris Suburbs for Free
(or Extremely Cheap)

There are many free or extremely cheap sights and activities in the Paris suburbs and surrounding Ile-de-France region, and many are accessible via public transportation. You can get to all the places in this chapter from Paris on the Métro, RER, and/or bus. The method of transport that puts you closest to the sight is listed first, followed by any alternate means. Reaching some sights will mean a ride on the Métro or RER combined with a bus trip.

Remember, RER travel outside Paris requires the purchase of a separate ticket or a pass for the zones in which you're traveling. Most tickets for suburban travel cost less than 20F for one-way, second-class seating.

Since public transportation rarely deposits you at the entrance of the sight, you'll have to walk from the station or bus stop. Fortunately, most suburbs have directional street signs to their important sights. To avoid getting lost, purchase Michelin's fold-out map #101, *Banlieue de Paris*, or a similar map showing the primary streets and sights of the destinations listed below.

Argenteuil—Monet & the Seine River
A few miles west of Paris on a wide loop of the Seine River, the industrial suburb of Argenteuil is where Monet painted several of his masterful boat and river scenes. If you're interested in his

work, it's a worthy pilgrimage. *Address:* exit from the RER station to the Pont d'Argenteuil. RER: Argenteuil (C-3).

Asnières-sur-Seine—Cimetière des Chiens
Bordering the Seine River next to the Pont de Clichy, a privately owned dog cemetery has thousands of tiny graves, each with an inscribed tribute. Clearly, dogs are very dear to many Parisians. A few other animals, including an ostrich and a lynx, are buried here as well. *Address:* Pont de Clichy. *Hours:* March 15-Oct 15: Wed-Mon 10-noon & 3pm-7pm; Oct 16-March 14: Wed-Mon 10-noon & 3pm-5pm. *Métro:* Gabriel-Péri (13B).

Bièvres—Musée Français de la Photographie
The history of French photography is presented through exhibits of over 15,000 cameras from 1910-45, darkroom equipment, and thousands of photographs and rare daguerreotypes. Occasionally, the museum exhibits famous photographers' work. *Address:* 78 rue de Paris (phone 69-41-10-60). *Hours:* daily 10am-noon & 2pm-6pm. *Métro/Bus:* Mairie d'Issy (12) plus bus 190A to the Rond-Point du Petit-Clamart stop. *Admission:* 15F.

Boulogne-Billancourt—Musée de Boulogne-Billancourt
The industrial suburb of Boulogne-Billancourt abutting the 16th arrondissement was a favorite residence of 1930's artists seeking cheap rents. The city's small art museum features work by Gris, Denis, Bernard, Landowski (see below), and others. Several exhibits are devoted to architecture in the Paris area. *Address:* 26 avenue André-Morizet (phone 46-84-77-38). *Hours:* Wed-Sun 10am-noon & 2pm-5:30pm. *Métro:* Marcel-Sembat (9). *Admission:* 18F.

Boulogne-Billancourt—Musée Paul Landowski
This small museum has sculpture, documents, studies, and drawings by Paul Landowski (1875-1961), a prolific sculptor whose monumental works are found on squares in Paris and throughout the world. *Address:* 14 rue Max-Blondat (phone 46-84-77-37). *Hours:* Wed & Sat 10am-noon & 2pm-5:30pm; closed August. *Métro/Bus:* Porte d'Auteuil (10) plus bus 123 to Stade Roland Garros stop. *Admission:* 15F.

Boulogne-Billancourt — Jardins Albert-Kahn

A few blocks south of the Bois de Boulogne, there's a pretty park created in the 1920's by philanthropist and banker Albert-Kahn. It features an Oriental-style garden with footbridges, water lilies, rhododendrons, and flowers galore. *Address:* 1 rue des Abondances (phone 46-04-62-57). *Hours:* Tue-Sun 9am-6pm. *Métro:* Boulogne/Pont de St-Cloud (10). *Buses:* 52, 72. *Admission:* 12F.

Boulogne-Billancourt — Maison de la Nature & Musée Photothèque-Cinémathèque Albert-Kahn

Located next to the Jardins Albert-Kahn, this nature center offers a reference library about natural subjects and the environment, plus Kahn's photography and film collection (now owned by France). *Address:* 9-10 quai du 4-Septembre (phone 46-04-52-80). *Hours:* 9am-6pm for nature center and museum (temporary exhibitions only). *Métro/Buses:* same as Jardins Albert-Kahn. *Admission:* 22F.

Boulogne-Billancourt — Expo-Musée Renault

A series of exhibits and videos explains the history and manufacturing process of the renowned Renault automobile, which has been built in this city for several decades. *Address:* 27 rue des Abondances. *Hours:* Wed 2pm-6pm & Thur noon-6pm. *Métro/Buses:* same as Jardins Albert-Kahn.

Cergy-Pontoise — Sights of Pontoise

Pontoise's history began in the mid-800's, when a fortress was built here to protect Paris against invading Normans. Centuries later, it became a popular town, favored by the Kings of France and home to 19th-century artists Camille Pissarro and Paul Cézanne, who painted the nearby countryside. Today, merged with the modern city of Cergy, its narrow, twisting streets are an invitation into the past. Major sights left from the Middle Ages are the **Cathédrale St-Maclou** (circa 1140) and **Église Notre-Dame** (1060). The **Musée Tavet-Delacour**, housed in a 15th-century palace, features 20th-century art and a section devoted to Otto Freundlich, one of the first modern abstract artists, who was killed in the Maidanek concentration camp in 1943. The **Musée Pissarro**, housed in a manor house at the edge of a large park overlooking the Oise River, features paintings by Pissarro and exhibitions on themes in his work and on other artists who lived in the area. *Addresses:* Cathédrale St-Maclou: place du Petit-Martroy; Église Notre-Dame: rue Carnot; Musée Tavet-Delacour: 4 rue Lemercier (phone 30-38-02-40); Musée Pissarro: 17 rue du Château. *Hours:* Musée Tavet-Delacour: Wed-Mon 10am-noon & 2pm-6pm; Musée Pissarro: Wed-Sun 2pm-6pm. *RER:* Cergy-Préfecture (A-3). Pontoise is two miles north of the station. *Admission:* All sights are free except the Musée Tavet-Delacour, which is 20F.

Champigny-sur-Marne—Musée de la Résistance Nationale

The history of the French Resistance is presented through a series of documents, photographs, weapons, and other equipment used during World War II. Special emphasis is given to the participation of the French Communist factions. Despite the extra cost, this museum is well worth seeing, especially if you're a WWII buff. *Address:* 88 avenue Marx-Dormoy (phone 48-81-00-80). *Hours:* Mon & Wed-Fri 10am-5:30pm; Sat, Sun 2pm-6pm; closed Jan 1, May 1, July 14, Dec 25. *RER/Bus:* Champigny (A-2) plus bus 208. *Admission:* 25F.

Champs-sur-Marne—Château de Champs

The 18th-century château of Madame de Pompadour (mistress of Louis XV), set in a forest overlooking the Marne River, is one of the best examples of royal living on a smaller scale. Inside the château, sumptuous rooms are filled with art and furnishings from the period. The Chinese salon with ornamental panels is especially beautiful. *Address:* 31 rue de Paris (phone 60-05-24-43). *Hours:* May 1-Sep 31: Wed-Sun 10am-noon & 1:30pm-5:30pm; Oct 1-April 30: Wed-Sun 10am-noon & 1:30pm-4pm. *RER/Bus:* Bry-sur-Marne (A-4) plus bus 220 or 213B to the Champs-sur-Marne Mairie stop, or Noisiel (A-4) plus a one-mile walk. *Admission:* Carte Musées et Monuments.

Charenton—Musée Français le Pain

A half-mile south of the Bois de Vincennes in a working flour mill, this small museum is dedicated solely to bread. Its collection includes photographs, old *boulangeries* signs, recordings of songs discussing bread, cartoons, bread tax decrees, baking trays, ovens, copper molds, and dough sculpture. *Address:* 25 bis rue Victor-Hugo (phone 43-68-43-60). *Hours:* Tue & Thur

2pm-4:30pm; closed July 1-Sep 8. *Métro:* Charenton-Écoles (8). *Buses:* 24, 87, PC.

Between Châtou & Rueil-Malmaison—
Ile de Châtou

This long and narrow Seine River island was a favorite hangout of Courbet and the Impressionist artists Monet, Renoir, Seurat, and Sisley. Renoir's *Le Déjeuner des Canoiters* shows his friends lunching on the balcony of the Maison Fournaise, now a museum explaining its role in art history (25F). In later years, Van Gogh, Vlaminck, Derain, and Matisse would paint from this location, too. *Address:* steps lead to the island from the Pont de Châtou. *Hours:* open 24 hours. *RER:* Rueil-Malmaison (A-1) or Châtou-Croissy (A-1).

Ecouen—Musée National de la Renaissance

Set in a 42-acre forest on a hill outside the village of Ecouen, this 16th-century château-castle was built for the Count of Montmorency, who lived here from 1538 to 1555. In 1962, it became the national museum of Renaissance art, its 20 rooms filled with paintings, frescoes, tapestries, furniture, jewelry, and other priceless objects from the period. If you visit this sight, also stop in the village to see the 16th-century **Église St-Acceul**, with its massive tower and interesting stained glass windows. Some of the hiking trails in the statue-filled park and forest around the château provide shortcuts to the station. *Address:* Château d'Ecouen (phone 39-90-04-04). *Hours:* Wed-Mon 9:45am-12:30pm & 2pm-5:15pm. *Métro/Bus:* St-Denis-Porte de Paris (13) plus bus 268C to Ecouen/Ezanville Gare SNCF stop. *Admission:* 16F on Sunday.

Ivry-sur-Seine—Moulin de la Tour

One long block past the boulevard Périphérique, just outside the 13th arrondissement, you'll find a delightful restored windmill. *Address:* place du 8-Mai-1945 *Hours:* free guided tours 1st and 3rd Saturday of each month from 3pm-6pm. *Métro:* Porte d'Ivry (7). *Buses:* 82, PC.

Maisons-Laffitte—Château de Maisons-Laffitte

Bordering the Seine River a short distance north of the village of Maisons-Laffitte, this impressive château was built by Mansart from 1642 to 1650. It's the first building constructed by Mansart with high gabled windows built into a steep, four-sided roof—later known as a style of architecture (mansard). Although the château has changed ownership several times and the Musée du Louvre snatched most of its art collection, it offers some Gobelins tapestries, a print collection, and interesting *trompe-l'oeil* ceilings. Of special note: the views of a moat, a large reflecting pool, and a formal garden from its grand exterior staircase. *Address:* avenue Carnot (phone 39-62-01-49). *Hours:* Mon & Wed-Fri 9am-noon & 2pm-6pm, Sat 9am-noon & 2pm-4pm, Sun 2pm-6pm; closed Jan 1, May 1, July 14, Aug 15, Oct 1, Nov 11, Dec 31. *RER:* Maisons-Laffitte (A-3, 5). *Admission:* Carte Musées et Monuments.

Marne-la-Vallée—Euro Disney
The newest location of the world-famous amusement park and resort offers substantial discounts (50-75F reduction recently) from Jan 1 to March 31. Although the reduced prices still don't fit our "extremely cheap" guidelines, those of you with children will probably splurge anyway, so go during these months for big savings. For current prices, check with the Paris Office de Tourisme or an FNAC ticket outlet before leaving. *Address:* Parc Euro Disney (phone 49-41-49-10). *Hours:* June 21-Aug 31: daily 9am-11pm; Sep 1-June 20: 9am-9pm. *RER:* Marne-la-Vallée/Chessy (A-4). *Buses:* shuttle buses from both Paris airports connect Disney resort hotels. *Admission:* non-discounted prices are 195F for adults and 150F for children under 12.

Meudon-Val-Fleury—Villa des Brilliants et Musée Rodin
A few miles south of Paris is the house in which the sculptor Rodin spent the last years of his life. (He died in 1917.) He's buried here alongside his wife Rose Bluret, with a copy of *The Thinker* atop the grave. The museum annex contains original plaster casts, molds, sketches, and other items pertaining to his art. *Address:* 19 avenue Auguste-Rodin. *Hours:* Tue-Sun 9am-5pm. *RER:* Meudon-Val-Fleury (C-5, 7). *Admission:* 15F, Carte Musées et Monuments.

Meudon-Val-Fleury—Musée d'Art et d'Histoire
This small art and history museum in a charming 1676 house is dedicated to the famous artists and celebrities who lived in Meudon-Val-Fleury. The most notable works are sculpture by

La Grande Arche at La Défense

Arp, Bourdelle, and Stahly in the formal garden. Behind the museum, a building belonging to the Paris Observatory has a long terrace with fine views of Paris and the Seine River valley. *Address:* 11 rue des Pierres (phone 45-34-75-19). *Hours:* Tue-Sun 9am-5pm; closed Jan 1, May 1, July 14, Dec 25. *RER:* same as Maison d'Auguste Rodin Meudon. *Admission:* museum: 15F; terrace: free.

La Défense—La Défense & La Grande Arche

This is modern Paris at its best. Begun in 1967, when the Paris government relegated all new high-rise construction to the city outskirts, La Défense is now a self-contained city and a show-case of futuristic architecture and art. (Ask for the free brochure *Guide to the Works of Art in the La Défense District,* available at the information booth in front of the shell-shaped CNIT building.) Its newest focal point is **La Grande Arche**, a 25-story hollow cube (40F for elevator to the top) at its west end. It's aligned with the historic axis of the Arc de Triomphe/avenue des Champs Elysées/Luxor Obelisk (place de la Concorde)/Arc de Triomphe du Carrousel/Musée du Louvre.

Although it's mostly skyscrapers occupied by businesses, La Défense is also home to **Les Quatre Temps**, the largest shopping mall in Paris, with 260 stores, 20 restaurants, a supermarket, and nine movie theaters. On a rainy day when you're tired of museums, it's a great place to people-watch and shop for a souvenir. At least once a month, the mall hosts an antiques, crafts, or other kind of show. *Address:* Parvis de la Defense. *Hours:* Plaza area: open 24 hours; Les Quartre Temps: Mon 11am-8pm & Tue-Sat 10am-8pm (supermarket open to 10pm). *Métro/RER:* La Defense (1, A). *Bus:* 73. *Admission:* Grande Arche: Carte Musées et Monuments; all other sights free. (Some office and apartment buildings are closed to tourists.)

Neuilly-sur-Marne—Musée d'Art Brut

The Musée d'Art Brut features paintings, sculpture, and other works by artists who have had no formal training. Artists exhibited here who have gained respect and fame include Wölfi, Lonné, and Rattier. *Address:* 39 avenue du Géneral-de-Gaulle (phone 43-09-62-73). *Hours:* Thur-Sun 2pm-6pm. *RER:* Neuilly-Plaisance (A-4). *Admission:* 15F.

Neuilly-sur-Seine—Ile de la Jatte

Less than a mile north of La Défense, this long, narrow island in the Seine River was a favorite site of the Impressionist artists for painting—and partying. A few old houses and workshops from that era face the Neuilly side of the Seine, and there are parks on each end. *Address:* steps lead to it from the Pont de Levallois and Pont de la Grande Jatte. *Métro:* Pont de Levallois-Bécon (3). *Buses:* 82, 93.

Neuilly-sur-Seine—Musée de la Femme et Collection d'Automates

This privately owned museum features a unique collection of items pertaining to famous French women, including one of Marie Antoinette's corsets and over 30 automated dolls from the 19th-century. *Address:* 12 rue du Centre. *Hours:* Wed-Mon

2:30pm-5pm. *Métro:* Pont de Neuilly (1). *Buses:* 43, 73. *Admission:* 12F on Sunday.

Poissy—Sights of Poissy

The industrial suburb of Poissy, home to a large Citroën automobile factory, is also a historic town featuring the **Église Notre-Dame**, a 12th-century Romanesque church rebuilt with Gothic features in the 15th century and renovated by Viollet-le-Duc in the 19th. Other sights include the **Musée d'Histoire**, which documents the history of Poissy from Merovingian times to the present; the **Musée du Jouet**, a toys and games museum; the fortified entrance and only remains of an **ancient abbey**, now fronting a park along the Seine River; and the **Villa Savoye**, a square white house on concrete cylindrical piles built in 1931 by Le Corbusier for a local industrialist. *Addresses:* Musée d'Histoire: 12 rue St-Louis (phone 39-65-06-06); Église Notre-Dame: across from museum; Musée du Jouet: rue de la Tournelle. Abbey: behind Musée du Jouet via path; Villa Savoye: 82 rue de Villiers, past abbey in park (phone 30-74-60-65). *Hours:* Musée d'Histoire and Musée du Jouet, Wed-Sun 10am-5:30pm; Villa Savoye: Nov 1-March 30: Mon, Wed-Sat 10am-5pm. *RER:* Poissy (A-5). *Admission:* museums 20F; all other sights are free.

Rueil-Malmaison—Musée National des Châteaux de Malmaison et Bois-Préau

Near the small village of Rueil-Malmaison, two separate châteaux have museums devoted to the history of Napoléon Bonaparte and his wife (until their 1809 divorce), the Empress Josephine. The museum in the **Château Malmaison**, where Josephine lived until her death in 1814, features Napoléon's personal library, Josephine's bedroom and clothes, paintings, sculpture, furniture, decorative art, and other exhibits about their erstwhile love affair. The museum in the smaller **Château Bois-Préau** deals with Napoléon's exile on St. Helena, with exhibits of his clothes and other belongings, paintings of the emperor, a re-creation of his deathbed room, and newspapers documenting the return of his body to France. Both châteaux are set in lovely parks with lots of flowers, trees, statues, fountains, and paths. *Addresses:* Château Malmaison: 1 avenue du Château (phone 47-49-20-07); Château Bois-Préau: 1 avenue de l'Impératrice Josephine. *Hours:* Château Malmaison: Wed-Mon

10am-noon & 1:30pm-5pm; Château Bois-Préau: Wed-Mon 10:30am-12:30pm & 2pm-5:30pm. *Métro/Bus:* La Défense (1) plus bus 158A to Malmaison-Château stop. *RER:* Rueil-Malmaison (A-1) plus two-mile walk. *Admission:* 28F for entry to both museums, Carte Musées et Monuments, 12F for Château Bois-Préau only. On Sunday, Château Malmaison is 13F and Château Bois-Préau is 6F.

St-Cloud—Parc St-Cloud

From this pretty park, designed by Le Nôtre in 1760 and the former site of Napoléon III's palace (burned by the Prussians in 1870), there are fine views of the Seine River and west Paris. Lining its many paths are statues, fountains, and terraced flower gardens. At the northeast corner, see the **Grande Cascade**, a 296-foot manmade waterfall, and the **Grande Jet**, a 138-foot fountain. On the second and fourth Sunday of each month from May 1-Sep 1, the park hosts a special fountain display. (Check with Office de Tourisme for current times.) *Address:* west of Seine River between Pont de St-Cloud and Pont de Sèvres. *Hours:* daily 9am-8pm. *Métro:* Boulogne/Pont de St-Cloud (10), Pont de Sèvres (9). *Buses:* 52, 72. *Admission:* free for pedestrian traffic.

St-Cloud—Hippodrome St-Cloud

This is another popular horse-racing track with an extremely cheap admission price, except during its annual events, when seats are reserved far in advance. *Address:* north of Parc de St-Cloud off allée Chamillard. *Hours:* check sports pages for current races. *Métro/Bus:* Porte d'Auteuil (10) plus bus 244N to Suresnes Cité Jardins stop. The racetrack is just south. *Admission:* 20F for cheapest seats.

St-Denis—Cathédrale St-Denis

Although the current industrialized suburb of St-Denis is unexceptional, the Kings of France (beginning in the 6th century) chose the town's cathedral as their final resting place. Inside the choir end of the Romanesque cathedral and in the crypt under the main altar, you'll see the elaborately sculpted tombs of Clovis, Pepin the Short, François I, Henri II, Anne of Brittany, Catherine de Medici, Louis XII, and others, plus the burial vault of the Bourbon family, which includes the remains of Louis XVI and Marie Antoinette. Most of the bodies once contained here were exhumed and destroyed during the French Revolution. The cathedral also has some beautiful Gothic stained glass windows. *Address:* place de l'Hôtel-de-Ville. *Hours:* summer: daily 10am-7pm; winter: 10am-5pm; closed Jan 1, May 1, Nov 1, Nov 11, Dec 25. *Métro:* St-Denis-Basilique (13). *Admission:* Carte Musées et Monuments.

St-Denis—Musée d'Art et d'Histoire de la Ville de St-Denis

This combined art, archaeology, and history museum, housed in a former convent, features interesting paintings of industrial landscapes by 19th- and 20th-century artists, plus a large collection of documents, posters, cartoons, and other artifacts relating to the short-lived 1871 Commune. (St-Denis is a French Communist Party stronghold in France.) *Address:* 22 bis rue Gabriel-Péri (phone 42-43-05-10). *Hours:* Wed-Mon 10am-5:30pm. *Métro:* same as Cathédrale St-Denis. *Admission:* 20F.

St-Denis (to Paris)—Canal St-Denis

The canal skirting the south side of St-Denis enters Paris on the west side of La Villette by the Cité des Sciences et de l'Industrie. For a long (about three miles) but pleasant walk, follow the towpaths along the canal back to Paris. Barges still use the canal as a shortcut across the north side of Paris to the Seine River. *Address:* opposite St-Denis RER station and crossed by avenue Corentin Cariou in Paris. *Métro/RER:* St-Denis (D), Porte de la Villette (7), Corentin Cariou (7). *Buses:* 60, PC (at La Villette).

St-Germain-en-Laye—Musée des Antiquités Nationales

France's national archaeology museum displays objects discovered in France dating from the Stone Age to the 8th century, including a large Gallo-Roman section. One of the highlights is the oldest known representation of a woman's face. The museum is contained on three floors of the Château de St-Germain-en-Laye, a residence built in the 12th century for François I and later used as a country getaway by Louis XIV until he completed Versailles. A few miles west of Paris above a bend in the Seine River, the museum's terrace offers good views of the western suburbs of Paris. *Address:* place du Château (phone

34-51-53-65). *Hours:* Wed-Mon 9am-5:30pm. *RER:* St-Germain-en-Laye (A-1). *Admission:* 20F, Carte Musées et Monuments.

St-Germain-en-Laye—Musée du Prieuré

Housed in a 17th-century royal hospital that became the home and studio of modern artist Maurice Denis, this art museum features important paintings, sculpture, and posters by Denis, Gauguin, Sérusier, Vuillard, and other artists of the Symbolist and Nabi movements. Statues by Bourdelle are in the terraced garden. Students of modern art will want to visit this museum, despite its extra cost. *Address:* 2 bis rue Maurice-Denis (phone 39-73-77-87). *Hours:* Wed-Sun 10am-5:30pm. *RER:* same as Musée des Antiquités Nationales. *Admission:* 25F.

St-Mandé—Marché aux Vieux Papiers

If you collect old postcards, stamps, and letters, come to this once-a-week sale frequented by local collectors. But beware of counterfeit items! *Address:* avenue de Paris. *Hours:* Wed 10am-6pm. *Métro:* St-Mandé Tourelle (1). *Buses:* 46, 56, 86.

St-Ouen—Marché aux Puces de la Porte de Clignancourt

Just outside the boulevard Périphérique, the largest flea market in metropolitan Paris bursts with over 3,000 stalls and a few buildings selling everything from used clothes to cheap ceramics to valuable antiques. Numerous street vendors, lined from the Métro to the market, offer more goods for sale. Some prices for items are extremely cheap, while antiques can be outrageously expensive. (My wife bought a slightly used leather purse here for 20F, while I bought a used wool sweater for 10F.) Come for the experience and get elbow-to-elbow with Parisians digging for bargains. *Address:* outside boulevard Périphérique between porte de Clignancourt and porte de St-Ouen. *Hours:* Fri-Mon 8am-8pm. *Métro:* Porte de Clignancourt (4), Porte de St-Ouen (13). *Buses:* 56, 85, PC.

Sceaux—Musée de l'Ile-de-France & Parc de Sceaux

Housed in a small 19th-century château a few miles south of Paris, this interesting museum documents the history of the

Ile-de-France region (the geographic and government region surrounding Paris). Its collection includes paintings, ceramics, costumes, tapestries, furnishings, and models of châteaux found in the region. The large park connected to the château, created in 1670 with a Grand Canal, reflecting basin, fountains, statues, sculpted shrubbery, and crisscrossing lanes, is considered one of the finest designed by Le Nôtre. In addition, outdoor chamber music and rock concerts are held here every summer (expensive). *Address:* Château de Sceaux (phone 46-61-06-71). *Hours:* Museum: Mon & Fri 2pm-5pm; Wed, Thur, Sat, & Sun 10am-noon & 2pm-5pm; Park: open daily, sunrise to sunset. *RER:* Bourg la Reine (B-4; closer to museum entrance), Parc de Sceaux (B-4). *Admission:* 22F for museum (15F on Sunday), free for park.

Sèvres—Musée Nationale de la Céramique
The small city of Sèvres is world-renowned for fine porcelain and ceramics. Its national ceramics museum displays several pieces created by the Royal Porcelain Factory from 1738 to the present, plus a fine collection of china, pottery, and porcelain objects from other countries. To explain the manufacturing process, audio-visual presentations run daily, and there are demonstrations by craftsmen on the first and third Thursday of each month. *Address:* place de la Manufacture; across Seine River from Métro station (phone 45-34-99-05). *Hours:* Wed-Mon 10am-5:15pm. *Métro:* Pont de Sèvres (9). *Admission:* Carte Musées et Monuments.

Suresnes—Mont Valérien Cimetière et Mémorial National
This memorial and cemetery, set atop a high hill, remembers 4,500 hostages and Resistance members executed by the Nazis at this site from 1940 to 1944. Although the memorial is rather spare (a squat Lorraine cross in brick with eight bas-reliefs on each side), there are lovely views of the Bois de Boulogne and Paris in the distance. *Address:* rue Paul-Vaillant-Couturier. *Hours:* daily 8am-6pm. *Métro/Bus:* Porte d'Auteuil (10) plus bus 244N to Suresnes Longchamp/SNCF stop.

Versailles—Palais de Versailles
One of the most awesome sights in France, the Palace of Ver-

Statues in the Apollo Basin on the grounds of the Palais de Versailles.

sailles was the residence of the Kings of France from 1682 to 1789. From the luxuriously designed and furnished living quarters to the meticulously tailored landscape of statue-lined paths, fountains, forests, canals, and gardens, Versailles demonstrates wealth spent to the extreme. Due to its size, you'll need at least two days (some people take four) to see everything carefully: the palace, Petit Trianon, Grand Trianon, Marie Antoinette's hamlet, and the grounds. But don't miss it, even if you must cram it all in during one day. *Address:* end of avenue de Paris; follow the crowds from the station (phone 39-50-58-32). *Hours:* summer: Tue-Sun 9am-7pm; winter: Tue-Sun 9am-5:30pm. *RER:* Versailles-Rive Gauche (C-5). *Admission:* Sunday: Carte Musées et Monuments.

Annual Free (or Extremely Cheap) Events in Paris and Its Suburbs

Before you make plans to attend these events, be sure to contact the festival organizers or the French Government Tourist Office for exact dates, times, and ticket prices. If you're in Paris, check the newspaper or weekly current events magazines.

At press time, all of the listed events fit the free or extremely cheap categories, but, of course, ticket prices are subject to change. Locations mentioned below, unless otherwise noted, are discussed in the arrondissement chapters, where you'll find their addresses.

January

First weekend—Russian Orthodox Christmas
Gather with the local Russian community in the Cathédrale St-Alexandre-Nevsky for this unique celebration, featuring a procession of priests dispensing incense from swinging lanterns. Vespers: 6pm on Saturday; mass: 10am on Sunday. Free.

Sunday closest to the 21st—Commemorative Mass for Louis XVI
For a unique and somber service, attend mass in the Chapelle Expiatore with descendants and fans of King Louis XVI to mourn his January 21, 1793 beheading. Free.

February

Sunday closest to the 15th—Chinese New Year Festival
In the 13th arrondissement, join the local Asian population in Paris to watch parades and martial arts demonstrations, sample food, and attend other festivities. Most activities occur along the avenues d'Ivry and Choisy. Free.

All month—Foire à la Feraille de Paris
This antiques and bric-a-brac fair is held in the Parc de Floral of the Bois de Vincennes. Free for browsing.

March

All month—Festival des Instruments Ancien
This festival celebrates music from past centuries, played on antique instruments in churches and music halls throughout Paris. Extremely cheap tickets.

All month—Foire du Trone
The Foire du Trone is a gigantic carnival and amusement park, with roller coasters, pony rides, fortune tellers, fun houses, and enough caramel apples, cotton candy, and waffles to keep junk-food addicts happy for days. It runs 2pm-midnight along the Pelouse de Reuilly (southwest corner) in the Bois de Vincennes. Free entry.

Late March/early April—Festival International: Films des Femmes
This festival is dedicated to women in film and films by women. Tickets are cheap, and you can vote for the awards. It's held in the suburb of Créteil. (By Métro, travel to the Créteil-Préfecture station, line 8.) For exact dates, contact the Maison des Arts, place Salvador-Allende, 94000 Créteil (phone 49-80-18-88).

April

1st—April Fool's Day
Throughout the day, you'll see pranksters sticking paper sea monsters on people's backs. French bakers make the day more festive by creating breads, cakes, and chocolate in the shape of fish. Join the fun!

April 1st through Oct. 30th—Son et Lumière des Invalides
A sound and light show (separate English and French versions) occurs in the courtyard of the Hôtel des Invalides every night. Free.

Early April—Mardi Gras
Although Paris's version of Mardi Gras (held the last week of Lent) is not as wild as the celebrations in other parts of the world, it still features colorful parties and parades. Free.

Last three Sundays—Buddhist New Year Fête
France's Buddhist population gathers for prayer and festivity at the Buddhist Temple in the Bois de Vincennes. Free.

Late April through Oct.—Shakespeare Garden Festival
The Bard's plays are performed in the Shakespeare Garden of the Pré Catalan section of the Bois de Boulogne by French and English theatrical groups. Tickets start at 30F.

Late April or mid-May—International Marathon of Paris
Thousands of professional and amateur runners start from place de la Concorde, set the pace up avenue des Champs-Élysées, then take a route through Paris, with the finish line at the Château de Vincennes. For the exact date and route, stop by Marathon (29 rue de Chazelles), a running equipment shop and sponsor. Free to watch.

May

1st—La Fête du Travail (national holiday)
On the French version of Labor Day, political parties and trade unions march and hold demonstrations in various parks throughout Paris. Although it can be interesting, exercise caution if you notice riot police. It's common for opposing factions to clash.

8th—Victory in Europe Day (national holiday)
To commemorate the end of World War II, there's a military parade down the avenue des Champs-Élysées, a ceremony at the Arc de Triomphe, and lots of veterans in the streets adorned with medals. Free.

May 1st through Sept. 30th—Grandes Eaux Musicales

A spectacular display of lights and sound occurs at the primary fountains on the grounds of the Palais de Versailles every Sunday from 4pm-6pm. Free with your palace entry ticket.

All month—Salon de Montrouge

This is the most important contemporary art exhibition for young artists, sculptors, and photographers. Out of 2,000 applicants, only 300 are selected for the show. The exhibition hall is just outside the boulevard Périphérique at 43 de la République in the suburb of Montrouge. (Take line 4 to the Porte d'Orléans Métro station or bus #68). Free.

June

Mid-month—Festival Foire St-Germain

This festival features an antiques fair in place St-Sulpice, concerts in the 6th arrondissement Mairie (78 rue Bonaparte), and sports events in the Jardin du Luxembourg. For exact dates, call 43-29-12-78. Free.

21st—Fête de la Musique & Summer Solstice Celebration

Fire-eaters, clowns, and other performers roam the streets, and you'll find street theater, parades, rock bands at place de la Bastille, chamber music at the Palais Royal, all-night dancing, and other amusements throughout Paris to celebrate the first day of summer. The Latin Quarter fills with anyone who can blow a horn, carry a tune, or watch others do so. Free.

22nd through Oct. 1st—International Rose Competition

After prizes are awarded on June 21, the public has access to the rose display held in the rose garden of the Parc de Bagatelle in the Bois de Boulogne. Free.

3rd Saturday—SOS Racisme concert

This concert and rally protests racism in France. Expect lots of young people, counter-protesters, and riot police. Free.

3rd or 4th weekend—Fêtes du Pont Neuf

For this festival, the oldest bridge in Paris and place Dauphine are closed to traffic and opened for dancing, music, street artists, and minstrels. Free.

28th—Fête du Cinema

For the price of one movie ticket, you can roam from theater to theater until your eyes get exhausted. It's a great deal if you can find enough movies you want to see. Tickets are sold at participating movie theaters.

Last week—Festival de la Butte Montmartre

Experimental drama, dance, and jazz performances dominate this festival. For details, contact the festival at 4 bis rue Ste-Isaure, 75018 Paris (phone 42-62-46-22). Many events are free.

Late June—Course de Garçons de Café

Once a year, 500 waitresses and waiters race in the streets of Paris with a tray holding one wine bottle and three glasses. Any spillage or breakage on the five-mile course disqualifies the entrant. The course starts and ends at the Hôtel de Ville. Free.

All month—Festival du Marais

Classical and jazz music, theater, and exhibits are held inside Hôtel Particulars and outside in the gardens and courtyards. The classical concerts are expensive, but the other events are free or extremely cheap. For details, contact the festival at 68 rue François-Miron, 74004 Paris (phone 45-23-18-25).

Sometime in June—Paris Cricket Tournament

The English sport of cricket has recently caught on in France. This tournament is held in the Terrain de Bagatelle section in the Bois de Boulogne. Check the sports page for exact dates. Free.

July

14th—Bastille Day (national holiday)

The liveliest and biggest national celebration of the year, Bastille Day commemorates the storming of the Bastille prison in 1789. The day starts with the army parading down the avenue des Champs-Élysées (with jets flying overhead) and ends with fireworks over the Arc de Triomphe, Montmartre, Parc Montsouris, Palais de Chaillot, and elsewhere. Traditional street dances are held on the eve of Bastille Day into the wee hours of the morning at the tip of the Ile St-Louis (the French Communist Party always throws its gala there), Hotel de Ville, place de la Contrescarpe, and of course, place de la Bastille, where it all began. Check the newspapers a few days before to see where other celebrations will take place. Free.

Mid-July through mid-Sept.—Festival Estival
The Paris summer festival features opera, chamber music, and recitals in churches, palaces, and concert halls throughout Paris. Tickets start at 25F. For details, contact the festival at 20 rue Geoffrey-l'Asnier, 75004 Paris (phone 48-04-98-01).

4th Sunday—Tour de France
Thousands of spectators line the avenue des Champs-Élysées to watch the finish of this month-long, 2,112-mile bicycle race. This is the biggest sporting event of the year in France, as significant as the World Series and Super Bowl championships in the U.S. The winner is considered the best racer in the world. Get there early and expect a huge crowd. Free.

August

15th—Fête de l'Assomption (national holiday)
With all its pomp and formality, the procession of the Feast of the Assumption of the Virgin Mary at the Cathédrale de Notre Dame is a magnificent sight. When the weather is good, mass is held outside on the plaza in front of the cathedral. Free.

September

1st weekend—Paris Triathlon
This endurance race (swimming, bicycling, and running) starts when the participants jump off the Pont de la Concorde into the Seine River. Free.

2nd or 3rd week—Fête de l'Humanité
The French Communist Party's annual fair is a unique event to attend. Over 100,000 people converge to hear debates, collect literature distributed by worldwide Communist party factions, and be entertained by the likes of Charlie Mingus, Marcel Marceau, the Bolshoi Ballet, and radical theater troupes. Party membership is not required to attend this event, which is held in the large suburban Parc Départemental de la Courneuve (one mile north of La Courneuve; take line 7 to 8-Mai-1945 Métro station). Free.

3rd Sunday—Portes Ouvertes Monuments Historiques

On this day, Hôtel Particuliers, private homes, archaeological digs, and government buildings in Paris are opened to the public. Get a list of the buildings (with admission information) from the Office du Tourisme or the Association Paris Historique, 44 rue François-Miron, Paris 75004 (phone 40-15-82-92).

Last two weeks—Festival de Musique de Chambre de Paris

This festival features chamber music concerts in the Hôtel Carnavalet and other historic buildings in Paris. Tickets start at 25F. For details, contact the festival at 5 bis, rue St-Gilles, 75003 Paris (phone 42-77-44-58).

Late Sept. through Dec.—Festival d'Automne

Art exhibits, drama, ballet, and chamber music performances are held in the Centre Georges Pompidou, other museums, and churches in Paris. Tickets start at 25F. For details, contact the festival at 156 rue de Rivoli, 75001 Paris (phone 42-96-96-94).

Late Sept. through Dec.—Fêtes d'Automne

This is a scaled-down version of the above festival, held only at 5th arrondissement cultural sites, with cheaper admissions.

All Sept., Oct., & Nov.—Festival d'Art Sacré

The Radio France Philharmonic Orchestra, Société de Musique Contemporaine, and other performers hold sacred music concerts in Paris churches throughout the fall. Tickets start at 15F. For details, contact the festival at 4 rue Jules-Cousin, 75004 Paris (phone 42-77-92-26).

October

Oct. or Nov.—Nouveau Beaujolais

When the newly harvested Beaujolais wine arrives in Paris, you'll find bars and cafés suddenly packed with people lining up for a taste of the year's vintage (best consumed when the wine is very young). Some people leave work to be among the first to get a sample. Extremely cheap at some establishments.

1st Saturday—Fête des Vendanges à Montmartre

This festival celebrates the harvest of Clos Montmartre, the only commercial vineyard left in Paris. Though it's hardly France's best wine, it still merits a celebration. The basement of the 18th arrondissement Mairie (1 place Jules Joffrin) becomes a winery, and there are parades and other festivities throughout the area. The vineyard is on rue Saules.

Early Oct.—Les 6 Heures Motonautiques de Paris
A thrilling six-hour speedboat race is held on the Seine River. Check the sports pages for more details. Free.

First two weeks—Le Mondial de l'Automobile
Held in the Parc des Expositions, this show features the latest developments in the international automobile industry. Admission varies.

2nd Sunday—Rue Lepic Antique Automobile Race
Antique cars race along this winding and hilly Montmartre street. Free.

Mid-Oct.—Les 20km de Paris Race
Over 20,000 runners participate in a long-distance footrace that begins and ends at the Tour Eiffel. Free.

Late Oct. to early Nov.—Festival de Jazz de Paris
There's so much jazz in Paris music clubs that a yearly festival seems redundant, but this fest allows fans to see the biggest names together at one event. It's held at several different Paris concert halls. Although tickets start at 35F, there's a one-price pass that gets you into all the events (a great deal if you attend most of the concerts). For details, contact the festival at 211 avenue Jean-Jaurès, 75019 Paris (phone 40-56-07-17).

Sometime in Oct.—Génie de la Bastille
The artists in the Bastille area open their studios to the public for four days in October to show and sell their work. For the exact dates, contact the organizers at 71 rue du Faubourg-St-Antoine, 75011 Paris (phone 42-02-97-45).

November

11th—Armistice Day (national holiday)
In a special ceremony at the Arc de Triomphe, the Président, politicians, and other celebrities lay wreaths on the Tomb of the Unknown Soldier. Free.

Mid-Nov. through mid-Dec.—Festival Internationale de la Guitarre

Concerts by international guitarists are held in many Parisian churches. Tickets start at 15F. For details, call 40-30-10-13.

December

24th—Christmas Eve Mass

This is the only time of the year that the Cathédrale de Notre-Dame is packed, so get there early if you want a seat. Mass begins at midnight. Afterwards, many of the neighboring cafés stay open for anyone wanting to celebrate Christmas early. Free for mass.

31st—Fête de St-Sylvestre (New Year's Eve Celebration)

When the clock strikes midnight, Paris explodes in tumultuous celebration—strangers embrace, motorists find people dancing on their car hoods, and for a few hours, the boulevard St-Michel, avenue des Champs-Élysées, and other streets in Paris become pedestrian malls, much to the dismay of the police attempting to direct traffic.

Glossary of Commonly Used Terms & Names

allée—a street designation.

Baron Haussmann (Georges Eugène)—urban planner under Napoléon III who dramatically changed the look of Paris in the mid-19th century by replacing narrow streets with wide boulevards and leveling derelict neighborhoods

Beaux Arts—fine arts

boulevard—usually a multi-lane street

Carte Musées et Monuments—pass card to 65 museums and monuments in Paris and Ile de France region

Cathédrale—cathedral

centre—center

cours—a street designation, also a courtyard

Église—church

Hôtel—mansions built in the city for royalty, ministers, and the wealthy

Ile—island

Jardin—a finely designed park with flowers, hedges, fountains, and statues

King Louis XIII—reigned 1610-1643

King Louis XIV—reigned 1643-1715

King Louis XV—reigned 1715-1774

King Louis XVI—reigned 1774-1792

Métro—the city's subway system

Musée—museum

Napoléon (Bonaparte)—ruler/Emperor 1799-1814

Palais—palace

place—traffic intersection, often with open grassy or gravel area, fountain, or monument at its center

Pont—bridge

quai—street by river, canal, or other body of water

RER—express subway/suburban rail system

rue—street

square—a grassy, open space similar to *place* (not always square in shape) but with park-like facilities and usually located in a low-traffic area

Viollet-le-Duc (Eugène Emmanuel)—architect who restored most of France's medieval buildings and monuments during the 19th century

About the Author

Mark Beffart, a writer and photographer from Atlanta, Georgia, is the author of *France on the TGV: How to Use the World's Fastest Train to Get the Most out of France, Fodor's Pocket Atlanta, Citypack Atlanta,* and *Walking Tours of France.* He is a regular contributor to Fodor's travel guides and the author of over 200 national magazine articles about art, business, and travel. He is also a partner in an editorial services/newsletter design company.

More Great Books
from Mustang Publishing

Europe for Free by Brian Butler. If you're on a tight budget — or if you just love a bargain — this is the book for you! With descriptions of thousands of things to do and see for free all over Europe, you'll save plenty of lira, francs, and pfennigs. **$10.95**
 "*Forget about American Express. One of these books is what you shouldn't leave home without!*" — Toronto Sun

Also in this series:
London for Free by Brian Butler. **$9.95**
The Southwest by Greg & Mary Jane Edwards. **$9.95**
DC for Free by Brian Butler. **$9.95**
Hawaii for Free by Frances Carter. **$9.95**

France on the TGV: How to Use the World's Fastest Train to Get the Most out of France by Mark Beffart. Imagine boarding a train in Paris in the morning and arriving in Nice — almost 700 miles away — in time to get a suntan! With the TGV, the world's fastest train, it's easy, and this book describes everything you need to know to use this marvelous rail network. From descriptions of all the rail passes available to walking tours of over 50 French towns served by the TGV, it's a must for today's high-speed traveler. **$12.95**
 "*An exceptionally useful guide.*" — Atlanta Constitution

Northern Italy: A Taste of Trattoria by Christina Baglivi. For the most delicious, most authentic, and least expensive meals in Italy, skip the *ristoranti* and head straight for *trattorie,* the small, unassuming cafés known only to locals. Describing over 80 *trattorie* from Rome to Milan, it's a must for the hungry traveler. **$12.95**
 "*The book's general premise is as sound as its specific eatery recommendations.*" — N.Y. Daily News

The Complete Book of Golf Games by Scott Johnston. Want to spice up your next round of golf? With over 80 great betting games, side wagers, and tournament formats, this book will delight both weekend hackers and the totally obsessed. From descriptions of favorite games like Skins and Nassau to details on unusual contests like String and Bingo Bango Bongo, it's essential equipment in every golfer's bag. **$9.95**
> *"A must acquisition."*—Petersen's Golfing

How to Be a Way Cool Grandfather by Verne Steen. Some things a grandfather just *ought* to know: how to make a slingshot from an old limb and a rubber band, how to make a kite from a newspaper, how to do a few simple magic tricks, and how to make his grandchildren say, "Cool, Grandpa!" With complete details on making 30 fun, inexpensive toys, plus hints on using them to impart valuable lessons to kids, this is a great book for every old fogey who'd rather be way cool. **$12.95**
> *"A charming book."*—The Spokesman-Review

The Complete Book of Beer Drinking Games by Griscom, Rand, & Johnston. With over 500,000 copies sold, this book reigns as the imbiber's bible! From classic games like Quarters and Blow Pong to wild new creations like Slush Fund and Beer Hunter—plus numerous funny essays, cartoons, and lists—this book is a party essential! **$8.95**
> *"The 'Animal House' of literature!"*—Dallas Morning News

Mustang books should be available at your local bookstore. If not, send a check or money order for the price of the book, plus $3.00 shipping *per book,* to Mustang Publishing, P.O. Box 3004, Memphis, TN 38173 U.S.A. To order by credit card, call toll-free 800-250-8713 or 901-521-1406.

Allow three weeks for delivery. For rush, one-week delivery, add $3.00 to the total. *International orders:* Please pay in U.S. funds, and add $5.00 per book for Air Mail.

For a complete catalog of Mustang books, send $2.00 and a stamped, self-addressed, business-size envelope to Catalog Request, Mustang Publishing, P.O. Box 3004, Memphis, TN 38173 U.S.A.